Richest of Poor Men

THE
SPIRITUALITY
OF ST. FRANCIS
OF ASSISI

Richest of Poor Men

John R. H. Moorman

Our Sunday Visitor, Inc.
Huntington, Indiana 46750

Nihil Obstat:
Rev. Lawrence A. Gollner
Censor Librorum

Imprimatur:
✠ William E. McManus, D.D.
Bishop of Fort Wayne-South Bend
October 20, 1977

First published in Great Britain in 1977
by Darton, Longman & Todd, Ltd.,
85 Gloucester Road,
London SW7 4SU, England

This edition published by arrangement
with Darton, Longman & Todd, Ltd.

ISBN: 0-87973-693-3
Library of Congress Catalog Card Number: 77-92391

Cover Design by Eric Nesheim

First O.S.V. Printing, March 1978
Second O.S.V. Printing, October 1978

Published, printed and bound in the U.S.A. by
Our Sunday Visitor, Inc.
Noll Plaza
Huntington, Indiana 46750

CONTENTS

FOREWORD

In this book no attempt is made to tell the story of the life of St Francis, as this has been done so often. All that is attempted here is to describe certain aspects of his life and his personality and ideals, using mainly the sources written by himself, or by those who actually knew and loved him or who wrote about him shortly after his death. Most of these sources will be found in the *Omnibus of Sources*, edited by Fr Marion Habig, O.F.M. (Chicago, 1973). Earlier translations of most of these documents had been published in previous years, but some of them are now difficult to obtain. I have, in one or two places, slightly altered the English text either for the sake of greater clarity or for some other reason.

The title of this book is taken from a passage in Celano's *First Life* (76) where he calls Francis *'ditissimus pauper'*. This I have translated as 'richest of poor men'.

I wish to express my thanks to Fr Denis Marsh, S.S.F., who very kindly read my manuscript and made some most valuable suggestions. I would also like to thank The Franciscan Herald Press for having given me permission to quote passages from *The Writings of St Francis*, edited and translated by Placid Herman and Benen Fahy.

Durham. 4 October 1976   JOHN R. H. MOORMAN

7

CHRONOLOGY OF THE LIFE OF SAINT FRANCIS

(N.B. Some of the early dates must be regarded as conjectural)

1182	Francis born in Assisi. Son of Peter Bernardone and his wife, Pica. Baptised John, but nicknamed Francesco by his father.
1202	Francis taken prisoner in war against Perugia and spends a year in prison. This followed by serious illness.
1204	Sets out to fight in Apulia on behalf of the Pope; but sees vision at Spoleto and returns home.
1206	Undergoes what is known as his 'conversion'. Receives a message from the crucifix in church of San Damiano. Gives everything back to his father. Rebuilds church and lives with the lepers.
1208	Hears Gospel read in the church of St Mary of the Angels, or the Portiuncula, and sets out as itinerant preacher of penitence.
1208-9	Joined by first disciples.
1209	Writes Primitive Rule which he takes to Rome and receives the blessing of Pope Innocent III. This followed by preaching missions in Italy.

1212	Reception of St Clare at the Portiuncula.
1214-15	Journey to Spain.
1217	General Chapter of friars held in Assisi. Missions planned to Germany and other countries. Provinces set up and ministers appointed.
1219	Francis goes to Egypt and pays his visit to the Soldan.
1220	Francis returns to Italy and finds tension among the friars. Resigns leadership of the Order.
1221	Writes Rules for the friars and for members of the Third Order.
1223	Composes Second Rule in order to meet the needs of those who want some relaxations in the life of the friars. Midnight Mass at Greccio.
1224	Francis, on La Verna, receives Stigmata.
1225	Stays for a time at San Damiano and writes '*Canticle of the Sun*'.
1226	Suffers much from sickness and blindness. Crude attempts to cure him are of no avail. Is taken to Assisi, first to the house of the Bishop and then on to the Portiuncula. Dies there on 3 October.
1228	Canonisation of St Francis.
1230	Translation of his body to new basilica.

REFERENCES

W.　　　*The Writings of St Francis of Assisi,* translated by Benen Fahy (London, 1963)

S. P.　　*Speculum Perfectionis,* known in English as *The Mirror of Perfection.* See *St Francis of Assisi: his Life and Writings as recorded by his Contemporaries,* translated by Leo Sherley-Price (London, 1959)

3 Soc.　　*Legenda Trium Sociorum,* known as *The Legend of the Three Companions.* English translation by Nesta de Robeck in *Saint Francis of Assisi: Omnibus of Sources,* ed. Marion A. Habig (Chicago, 1973)

1 Cel.　　*The First Life of St Francis by Thomas of Celano,* translated by Placid Hermann (ibid.)

2 Cel.　　*The Second Life of St Francis by Thomas of Celano,* translated by Placid Hermann (ibid.)

Bon.　　*Major Life of St Francis,* translated by Benen Fahy (ibid.)

L. F.　　*The Little Flowers of St Francis,* translated by Thomas Okey (several editions)

N. F.　　*A New Fioretti: a Collection of early stories about St Francis of Assisi hitherto untranslated,* edited and translated by John R. H. Moorman (London, 1946)

1. FRANCIS

St Francis is a much-loved figure; but he was, in fact, a very terrifying person. This is due to the fact that he set himself to achieve an ideal which demanded immense courage and determination; and he could be very severe with anyone who tried to persuade him to take a rather smoother path. His ideal was to be 'conformed in every act with that of our Blessed Lord', which meant that he took every recorded word of Christ at its face value, and set himself to obey every command, however great the cost. His early biographer, Thomas of Celano, says that 'he set out upon the way of total perfection'; and so far did he get along that rugged road that Ernest Renan, the French historian, could describe him as 'after Jesus, the only perfect Christian'.

Francis set out alone and single-handed on his particular way of discipleship; but, after a few years, he was joined by others who admired what he was doing, and felt that they wished to do likewise. From then onwards the little band of itinerant preachers, living in total poverty and simplicity, dependent for their very existence on the charity of their fellow-men, grew so rapidly that, by the death of St Francis, some eighteen years later, the Order contained several thousand friars scattered over most countries of Europe. In this rapid growth lay the seeds of division, for it was impossible to ensure that the high standards which Francis and his first disciples had accepted, and which they were prepared to fight and to suffer for, were always maintained. Francis did his best, in the early years, to examine every aspirant; and he had no hesitation in refusing men who, he thought, would not be able to stand the strain. He was also ruthless in reprimanding any brother who failed in any way to conform to his ideals. Celano tells us of a brother who

> went in the winter to a certain nunnery on an errand of sympathy, not knowing the saint's strong will about not going on such visits. After the fact had become known to the saint, he made the brother walk several miles naked in the cold and deep snow. (*2 Cel.* 206)

Many similar stories have been recorded as Francis fought desperately for his ideal.

Francis knew that to live a life based on absolute obedience to every word of Christ would lead to great hardship and suffering and might easily end in an early and painful death. This was the price which he was prepared to pay. He could do this only because of his deep faith and his habit of continuous prayer. How he combined the practice of the presence of God with unflagging activity in caring for the souls of men is the secret of what might be called his 'spirituality'.

2. FRANCIS AND GOD

The Father

There must have been very few moments in the life of St Francis, especially after what is called his 'conversion', when he was not thinking about God. Every detail of his daily life demanded divine guidance and approval. Often he would become rapt or in ecstasy, when he would be quite unaware of what was happening around him, as if he were literally in some other place. Celano writes of him as being 'often suspended in such sweetness of contemplation that, caught up out of himself, he could not reveal what he had experienced because it went beyond all human comprehension'; and he goes on to tell a story of how Francis was once riding on an ass to a certain leper-house by a route which would take him through the city of Borgo San Sepolcro. He goes on:

From all sides men and women came to see him, wanting to touch him out of devotion to him. What then? They touched him and pulled him about and cut off little pieces of his tunic to keep. The man seemed insensible to all these things, and paid no attention to the things that happened, as though he were a lifeless corpse. At length they came to the place and, though they had long left the city behind, that contemplator of heavenly things, as though returning to himself from

15

some other place, solicitously enquired when they would come to the city. (*2 Cel.* 98)

Francis was, in a sense, perpetually in and out of heaven. At times he was completely absorbed in what he was doing on earth, whether it were preaching, or tending the lepers, or giving advice to his brethren; and then, perhaps without much warning, he would drift into contemplation of heavenly things and become completely lost to the things of this world. Celano tells us that, towards the end of his life, Francis appointed certain of the brothers to take charge of him so that he might 'direct his attention more fully to God, and, in frequent ecstasy, wander about and enter the workshops of the blessed mansions of heaven and present himself with an abundance of grace on high before the most kind and serene Lord of all things'. (*1 Cel.* 102) After such expeditions Celano says that 'he seemed like a new man, one from another world' (*1 Cel.* 82); and shows how the long hours spent in the presence of God led him to a kind of 'divine familiarity'. (*1 Cel.* 91)

Francis felt all the time the rival claims of a life given entirely to contemplation and a life given to preaching and the service of mankind. So great was his love of God, and his desire to live permanently in the 'workshops of the blessed', that he was very seriously drawn, on several occasions, to abandon his preaching and practical ministry and retire to a life of continuous meditation and intercession. The problem caused him so much distress and anxiety that, at an early stage in his ministry, he discussed it with his friends.

'Which do you think is better,' he said, 'that I should devote all my time to prayer, or that I should go about preaching? I am a poor and worthless religious. I have no education and I am inexperienced in speaking; I have received the gift of prayer rather than that of preaching . . . Prayer helps to purify the desires of the heart and unites a person to the one, true and supreme Good, while giving an increase in virtue. The labour of preaching allows dust to enter into the soul and involves a lot of distraction and relaxation of religious discipline. In prayer we talk to God and listen to him and live a life worthy of the angels, with the angels for our companions. When preaching we have to descend to the level of human beings and live among them as one of them, thinking and seeing and hearing and speaking about human affairs.' (*Bon. xii*, 1)

Francis felt too humble to try to solve this problem by himself, so he decided to send Masseo to two people whose judgement he greatly respected – Clare and Sylvester. Masseo saw each one separately, and each gave the same reply. When Masseo returned, Francis

received him with great charity: he washed his feet and prepared a meal for him. And after he had eaten, St Francis called Brother Masseo into the woods. And there he knelt down before Brother Masseo, and baring his head and crossing his arms, St Francis asked him: 'What does my Lord, Jesus Christ, order me to do?' Brother Masseo replied that Christ had answered both Brother Sylvester and Sister Clare and her companion and revealed that 'He wants you to go about the world preaching, because God did not call you for yourself alone but also for the salvation of others'. And then the hand of the Lord came over St Francis. As soon as he heard this answer and thereby knew the will of Christ, he got to his feet all aflame with divine power and said to Brother Masseo with great fervour: 'So, let us go, in the name of the Lord'. (*L.F.* 16)

Francis, therefore, lived a kind of dual life in which the 'middle wall of partition' between earth and heaven was very flimsy and fragile. For long periods he would retire to some lonely place – an island, or a lake, or a secluded cave, and eventually the rocky summit of La Verna – to spend the time alone with God in prayer and contemplation. Then he would return to a life of great activity, journeys all over Italy and into Spain, Egypt, and the Holy Land, preaching wherever he went, tending the sick and the leprous, guiding his brotherhood in all its difficulties and uncertainties, writing the Rule by which they were to live. But it would be a mistake to think that these two aspects of his life were separated from each other. In the midst of all this activity, carried out in the rigours of travelling everywhere on foot, begging his food, sometimes being mocked and ill-treated as a madman, often in dire sickness, Francis was never far from the mansions of the blessed and from the presence of the God whom he loved so dearly and whose love he so greatly cherished.

> The moment he heard the love of God being mentioned [wrote Bonaventura], he was aroused immediately and so deeply moved and inflamed that it seemed as if the deepest chord in his heart had been plucked by his words. He used to say that to offer the love of God in exchange for alms was generosity worthy of a nobleman, and that anyone who thought less of it than money was a fool. The incalculable worth of divine love was the only thing that could win the kingdom of heaven. He used to say: 'Greatly to be loved is his love who loved us so greatly'. (*Bon.* ix, 1)

So important to St Francis was this love of God that he wrote it into the early Rule of 1221 in these words:

> In that love which is God, I entreat all my friars, ministers and subjects, to put away every attachment, all care and solicitude, and serve, love, honour and

adore our Lord and God with a pure heart and mind. This is what he seeks above all else. We should make a dwelling-place within ourselves where he can stay, he who is the Lord God Almighty, Father, Son and Holy Spirit. (*W*. 48–9)

In response to God's love man must show, in every possible way, his love for God. Again in the Rule of 1221 (unfortunately omitted in the formal and official Rule) he wrote:

With all our hearts and all our souls, all our minds and all our strength, all our power and all our understanding, with every faculty and every effort, with every affection and all our emotions, with every wish and desire, we should love our Lord and God who has given and gives us everything, body and soul and all our life. It was he who created and redeemed us, and of his mercy alone he will save us; wretched and pitiable as we are, ungrateful and evil, rotten through and through, he has provided us with every good and does not cease to provide for us.

We should wish for nothing else and have no other desire; we should find no pleasure or delight in anything except in our Creator, Redeemer and Saviour; he alone is true God, who is perfect good, all good, every good, the true and supreme good, and he alone is good, loving and gentle, kind and understanding; he alone is holy, just, true and right; he alone is kind, innocent, pure, and from him, through him, and in him is all pardon, all grace, and all glory for the penitent, the just and the blessed who rejoice in heaven.

Nothing, then, must be kept back, nothing separate us from him, nothing come between us and him. At all times and seasons, in every country and place, every day and all day, we must have a true and humble faith, and keep him in our hearts, where we must love, honour, adore, serve, praise and bless, glory and acclaim, magnify and thank, the most high, supreme and eternal God, Three and One, Father, Son and Holy Spirit, Creator of all and Saviour of those who believe in him, who hope in him, and who love him; without beginning and without end, he is unchangeable, invisible, indescribable and ineffable, incomprehensible, unfathomable, blessed and worthy of all praise, glorious, exalted, sublime, most high, kind, lovable, delightful and utterly desirable beyond all else, for ever and ever. (*W*. 51–2)

One of the things which helped Francis to feel the closeness of God was his ability to see God in all that was lovely or majestic.

In everything beautiful [wrote Bonaventura] he saw him who is beauty itself, and he followed his Beloved everywhere by his likeness imprinted on creation. (*Bon*.ix,1)

Just as Francis wanted, above all things, to give praise to God, so he called on all God's created things to join in this praise.

Much has been written about the great 'Canticle of the Sun' which Francis wrote towards the end of his life when he was lying, blind and in great suffering, both physical and mental, in a little hut in the garden of the Poor Clares at San Damiano just outside Assisi. No one can say for certain whether Francis was calling upon man to praise God for all his creation, or whether he was exhorting all the creatures to give praise to God. The Italian word *per* which he uses is ambiguous, as it can mean either 'for' or 'by'. Whichever way we take it, the Canticle is intended to draw together all creation in the ceaseless praise which must ascend, at all times, from earth to heaven.

> Most High, Almighty, good Lord,
> Thine be the praise, the glory, the honour
> and all blessing.
> To thee alone, Most High, are they due,
> And no man is worthy to speak thy Name. (*S.P.* 120)

He then calls upon Sun, Moon and Stars, and the four elements of Earth, Air, Fire and Water, to join in this praise. It is perhaps curious that, apart from a vague reference to 'all thy creatures', everything which he invokes is inanimate. There is no call to animals, birds, flowers, or even men (except in the penultimate stanza which was added later). Francis is really concerned here with the universe and the elements of which it is composed. What he is trying to do is to emphasise the grandeur and the wonder of God himself. If sun, moon and stars, shining around us, are objects of awe and reverence, how much greater must be the glory of the Lord which shines around his children.

Francis's intense interest in the living things of creation comes out elsewhere in his writings and in the story of his life. That Francis was a great lover of all created things (not only those most attractive to man) is well known; but in order to understand Francis's attitude to nature we need to see that this was founded upon two conceptions – one, that anything created by God should remind us of God because it belonged to him; the other, that certain things were worthy of our special love and reverence because they symbolised aspects of the nature and activity of God.

Francis saw everything created by God as part of his craftmanship and as one of his possessions. There are, as we know, many very charming stories of his love for the creatures by which he was surrounded – animals and birds, flowers and trees – and it is this aspect of his personality which has proved so attractive to men and women of this century. But it is easy to get this out of proportion. Francis certainly preached to the birds on several occasions; but this was to him of far less importance than his preaching to men to save them from their sins. Francis rescued lambs from the slaughter; but it was far more important to him to rescue lepers from rotting to death uncared for by their fellow-men. Francis calmed and tamed the savage wolf of Gubbio; but he was much more concerned to tame and pacify the backbiting and quarrelsome men and women in the Italian cities through which he passed.

But although we must be careful not to be led away into thinking that Francis was primarily a nature-lover, a suitable patron saint of animal welfare societies and pets' services, we know that he had a great devotion for all living things, and a great tenderness towards them just because they were made by God and belonged to him. 'We who were with him', wrote one of the friars, 'have seen him take inward and outward delight in almost every creature; and when he handled or looked at them his spirit seemed to be in heaven rather than on earth.' (*S.P.* 118). 'Every creature', Francis once said, 'proclaims "God made me for your sake, O man".' (ibid.)

This feeling of close affinity with nature moved Francis to great tenderness. He loved to rescue creatures which would otherwise have been put to death; he made friends with falcons and cicadas; he sang duets with a nightingale; he fondled hares, pheasants and waterfowl. In some strange way Francis, like many other saints before him, was able to create a relationship with an animal founded on mutual trust and affection. The same sort of affinity was felt for trees, which he hated to see felled, and for fire, which he would never willingly put out.

It is not surprising [says the *Mirror of Perfection*] that

fire and other creatures sometimes obeyed and revered him, for we who were with him often saw how much he loved them, and what pleasure he took in them. Indeed, his spirit was stirred by such love and compassion for them that he would not allow them to be treated without respect. He used to speak to them as if they were rational creatures with such inward and outward joy that at times he was rapt in ecstasy. (*S.P.* 115)

The other important thing to realise about St Francis's contact with nature is that he saw so many things as symbols of God. He always walked very tenderly over rocks because they reminded him of 'that rock which was Christ'. He had a particular affection for lambs because they symbolised the Lamb of God, the Christ. Trees were symbols of the cross, lights represented the Light of the World, flowers were connected with the lilies and roses of the Song of Songs, worms had to be picked up and taken to safety because the Psalmist called himself 'a worm and no man'. Thus everything in the natural world led Francis's mind and heart to God.

Living almost entirely in the open air, surrounded all the time by the works of God in nature, stimulated to ecstasy by the sight of a living creature or by some inanimate object which reminded him of its Creator, Francis was at all times very close to the heavenly places. The indescribable glory of God and the depth of his love and goodness were ever present in his mind, calling upon him and all men to give praise and thanksgiving.

After the awe-inspiring events on La Verna in 1224, when Francis received the wounds of Christ in his own body, his close friend, Brother Leo, who was at the time suffering from great sadness, hoped very much that the saint would write something encouraging for him. He did not dare to ask Francis to do this; but Francis sensed his need and said: 'Bring me some parchment and ink for I want to write down the words of the Lord and his praises which I have meditated upon in my heart'. This is what Francis wrote:

Thou art holy, Lord God, who alone workest wonders. Thou art strong. Thou art great. Thou art most high. Thou art the almighty King, Thou, holy Father, King of heaven and earth. Thou art the Lord God, Triune and One; all good. Thou art good, all good, highest good, Lord God living and true. Thou art charity, love. Thou art wisdom. Thou art humility. Thou art patience. Thou art security. Thou art quietude. Thou art joy and gladness. Thou art justice and temperance. Thou art all riches to sufficiency. Thou art beauty. Thou art meekness. Thou art protector. Thou art guardian and defender. Thou art strength. Thou art refreshment. Thou art our hope. Thou art our faith. Thou art our great sweetness. Thou art our eternal life, great and admirable Lord, God Almighty, merciful Saviour. (*Writings of St Francis*, ed. Paschal Robinson, 148–9)

Leo kept this scrap of parchment until his death. It can now be seen, just as Francis wrote it, in the great church in Assisi.

The Son

To God the Father endless praise should be offered. It is he who has made us and the universe in which we live. It is he who loves us with a love past all understanding, and who demands our love in return. This was basic to Francis's spiritual life.

His relationship with Christ, the Son, was more intimate and more personal. 'No man has seen God at any time'; but a number of people saw Jesus of Nazareth and reported on his words and works, so that it is possible to form a mental picture of what he was like. To Francis, the Son was adorable because he had shared our nature, had been one of us, because he had been 'tempted like as we are', because he had 'emptied himself and had taken the form of a servant, humbling himself and being obedient even unto death, the death of the cross'. As Francis wrote in his 'Letter to all the Faithful':

> How glorious, how holy and wonderful it is to have a Father in heaven. How holy it is, how beautiful and lovable to have in heaven a Bridegroom. How holy and beloved, how pleasing and lowly, how peaceful, delightful, lovable and desirable above all things it is to have a Brother like this, who laid down his life for his sheep. (*W*. 96)

Francis read the Gospels with great fervour and diligence. Everything that Jesus said or did was of the utmost importance to him since he wished to follow and obey him in every detail. Christ was his exemplar and model; and he wanted to live as he imagined Jesus had lived and do the things that Jesus did. He wanted to be despised and reviled; he wanted to have nowhere to lay his head; he would like to have been crucified, for he wanted above all things to lay down his life for Christ and his fellow-men.

What are sometimes known as the 'hard sayings' of Christ presented no problem to him. Jesus is reported to have said that it was a blessing to be poor and hungry, that it was better to weep than to laugh, and that it was a good thing when people hate you and exclude you from their company. When we read these words we realise, perhaps with some shame, that these are not the sort of things which we normally regard as desirable. We may not be money-grubbers, but we like to have enough to

25

live on. We may not be gluttons, but we want enough to eat. We may not be hedonists, but we want to enjoy life and be happy. We may not be sycophants, but we like the respect and esteem of our neighbours. Not so St Francis. To him poverty was an ideal to be sought at all costs; hunger was an offering to God; he wept so much that he went blind; he knew that when he was rejected and reviled he was being true to his profession. So it was with everything that Christ said. If he was reported as telling people to renounce everything that they possess-ed, to give to anyone that begged from them, to take no thought for the morrow, and to take up the cross and follow him, then Francis regarded these as his marching orders, to be obeyed literally and without argument or compromise. 'Obey the voice of the Son of God,' he wrote in a letter to the friars; 'keep his commandments whole-heartedly and practise his counsels with all your minds.' (*W.* 104)

Francis lived with the image of Jesus always before his eyes and the words of Jesus always in his ears.

No human tongue [wrote Bonaventura] could describe the passionate love with which Francis burn-ed for Christ, his Spouse. He seemed to be completely absorbed by the fire of divine love like a glowing coal. . . The memory of Christ Jesus crucified was ever present in the depths of his heart like a bundle of myrrh, and he longed to be wholly transformed into him by the fire of love. . . He loved Christ so fervently, and Christ returned his love so intimately, that he seemed to have his Saviour before his eyes continually, as he once privately admitted to his companions. (*Bon.* ix, 1–2)

So Francis walked with Christ, watching his every move and listening to his every word. 'Surely he was the most Christlike of men,' wrote Bonaventura; 'his only desire was to be like Christ and to imitate him perfectly.'

But if, to Francis, Christ was the perfect example of how a man should live, he was also the incarnate Son of God, the Word made Flesh, an object of adoration and praise.

To all the friars, so reverend, so well-beloved, [he wrote] Brother Francis, the least of your servants, worthless and sinful, sends greetings in him who redeemed and cleansed us in his most precious blood. At the sound of his name you should fall to the ground and adore him with fear and reverence, the Lord Jesus Christ, Son of the Most High, is his name, and he is blessed for ever. Amen. (*W.* 103–4)

Just as, with thoughts of God the Father, Francis was liable to be carried away into the rapture of contemplation, so it was with the name of Jesus.

When he pronounced the word 'Jesus' [says Bonaventura] or heard someone say it, he was filled with joy and he seemed to be completely transformed, as if he had suddenly tasted something marvellous or caught the strain of a beautiful harmony. (*Bon.* x, 6)

An example of this occurred at the celebration of the Nativity at Greccio in 1223, when Francis preached to the people and

spoke charming words concerning the nativity of the poor King and the little town of Bethlehem. Frequently too, when he wished to call Christ 'Jesus' he would call him simply the 'Child of Bethlehem', aglow with overflowing love for him; and speaking the word 'Bethlehem', his voice was more like the bleating of a sheep. His mouth was filled more with sweet affection than with words. Besides, when he spoke the name

27

'Child of Bethlehem' or 'Jesus' his tongue licked his lips, as it were, relishing and savouring with pleased palate the sweetness of the words. (*1 Cel.* 86)

Just because Francis lived so close to Jesus it is, perhaps, surprising to learn that there were times when the Master seemed far away and unapproachable. This was, no doubt, due to Francis's humility and sense of unworthiness. He felt himself continually surrounded by, and in conflict with, hosts of devils who tried to come between him and Christ and undermine his confidence. So it was that, after a long period of diabolic persecution in a little chapel on La Verna, Francis

> came out of the church and entered into a forest that was nearby. And there he gave himself to prayer. And praying and weeping and beating his breast, he sought Jesus Christ, the spouse and delight of his soul. And at last he found him in the secret depths of his heart. And he spoke to him reverently as to his Lord. Then he answered him as his Judge. Next he entreated him as a father. Then he talked with him as with a friend. (First Consideration on the Stigmata)

The words 'at last' are significant. Nothing in Francis's life was easy. Even contact with his beloved Jesus was sometimes to be made only by great perseverance and determination.

Francis had no doubt that, not only at crucial moments in his life but also in his day-to-day movements, Christ was leading him, talking to him, telling him what to do. The first great event of this kind was when, at Spoleto, he was told to abandon his knightly journey to Apulia, and the second when the crucifix spoke to him in the little ruined church of San Damiano.

While he was walking near the church, an inner voice

bade him go in and pray. He obeyed; and kneeling before an image of the crucified Saviour, he began to pray most devoutly. A tender, compassionate voice then spoke to him: 'Francis, do you not see that my house is falling into ruin? Go and repair it for me'. Trembling and amazed Francis replied: 'Gladly I will do so, Lord'. He had understood that the Lord was speaking of that very church which, on account of its age, was indeed falling into ruin. (*3 Soc.* 13)

It was not long, of course, before Francis realised that when Christ spoke of 'repairing the church' he was not talking about San Damiano or any other building, but of the whole Church which was sorely in need of renewal. But he never had the slightest doubt that, through the picture of the crucified Saviour, painted on a wooden cross, Christ himself had spoken to him and directed his footsteps. Shortly afterwards, in the church of St Mary of the Little Portion, when he still felt uncertain as to how he was to set about repairing Christ's Church, the Lord spoke to him through the reading of the Gospel. It was the feast of St Matthias and the Gospel for the day told how Christ sent out his disciples to preach.

Francis, hearing that the disciples of Christ should not possess gold or silver or money, nor carry along the way scrip, or wallet, or bread, or a staff; that they should not have shoes, or two tunics; but that they should preach the Kingdom of God and penance, immediately cried out exultingly: 'This is what I wish; this is what I seek; this is what I long to do with all my heart'. Then the holy father, overflowing with joy, hastened to fulfil that salutary word he had heard, nor did he suffer any delay to intervene before beginning devoutly to perform what he had heard. (*1 Cel.* 22)

And so it was all through his life. Sometimes the

message came through the reading of Scripture;
sometimes a voice was heard, sometimes a thought came
into his mind. But, whatever the means, Francis had not
the slightest doubt that Christ was constantly speaking
to him, encouraging him, giving him the power to fulfil
all that he had set himself to do in his life of total and un-
compromising obedience.

> Christ [writes Bonaventura], the Power of God and
> the Wisdom of God, whom the Spirit of God had
> anointed, was with his servant Francis in everything
> that he did, lending him eloquence in preaching sound
> doctrine and glorifying him by the extraordinary
> power of his miracles. (*Bon.* xii, 7)

Francis was, naturally, immensely moved by the
events which surrounded the birth and the death of
Jesus. He meditated at length on the scene of the Nativity, which reminded him both of the humility of the Son of
God, leaving the courts of heaven for the hardships,
sorrows, and sufferings of human life, and also of the
poverty into which he was born in the dirt, darkness and
discomfort of the stable.

> The birthday of the Child Jesus [writes Celano] Fran-
> cis observed with inexpressible eagerness over all other
> feasts, saying that it was the feast of feasts, on which
> God, having become a tiny infant, clung to human
> breasts. Pictures of those infant members he kissed
> with thoughts filled with yearning, and his compas-
> sion for the Child flooded his heart and made him
> stammer words of sweetness after the manner of in-
> fants. His name was like honey and the honeycomb in
> Francis's mouth. When the question arose about
> eating meat that day, since that Christmas day was a
> Friday, he replied, saying to Brother Morico: 'You
> sin, brother, calling the day on which the Child was

30

born to us a day of fast. It is my wish', he said, 'that even the walls should eat meat on such a day, and if they cannot, they should be smeared with meat on the outside'. On this day Francis wanted the poor and the hungry to be filled by the rich, and more than the usual amount of grain and hay given to the oxen and asses. (*1 Cel.* 199–200)

The story of how Francis celebrated Christmas at Greccio is well known. Anxious to teach people, not so much by word as by action, about the circumstances of Christ's birth, he got a friend to prepare a stable like the one at Bethlehem in which a Mass could be said in honour of the Christ Child.

If you want us to celebrate the present feast of our Lord at Greccio [he said] go with haste and diligently prepare what I tell you. For I wish to do something that will recall to memory the little Child who was born in Bethlehem and set before our bodily eyes in some way the inconveniences of his infant needs, how he lay in a manger, how, with an ox and an ass standing by, he lay upon the hay where he had been placed. (*1 Cel.* 84)

Large numbers of friars arrived and joined with the peasants of the neighbouring country in this midnight Mass, where 'simplicity was honoured, poverty was exalted, humility was commended, and Greccio was made, as it were, a new Bethlehem'. This dramatisation of the meaning of the incarnation was just the sort of thing which gave Francis immense pleasure. No wonder Celano can tell us that 'the saint of God stood before the manger, uttering sighs, overcome with love, and filled with a wonderful happiness'. (*1 Cel.* 85) It was, as we should expect, the fact that Christ had chosen to be born in poverty which appealed most to St Francis. As he wrote in his 'Letter to all the Faithful':

Our Lord Jesus Christ is the glorious Word of the Father, so holy and exalted, whose coming the Father made known by St Gabriel the Archangel to the glorious and blessed Virgin Mary, in whose womb he took on our weak human nature. He was rich beyond measure and yet he and his holy Mother chose poverty. (*W*. 93)

Meditation upon the circumstances of Christ's birth was naturally mingled with Francis's devotion to the obedience and love of the Virgin Mary.

Toward the Mother of Jesus [we are told] he was filled with an inexpressible love because it was she who made the Lord of Majesty our brother. He sang special Praises to her, poured out prayers to her, offered her his affections, so many and so great that the tongue of man cannot recount them. (*2 Cel*. 198)

The 'special Praises' which Celano mentions are known as the 'Salutation of the Blessed Virgin' and have survived as one of the authentic works of the saint.

Hail, holy Lady, most holy Queen, Mary, Mother of God, ever Virgin; chosen by the most holy Father in heaven, consecrated by him, with his most holy, beloved Son and the Holy Spirit, the Comforter. On you descended, and in you still remains, all the fulness of grace and every good. Hail, his palace; hail, his tabernacle; hail, his robe; hail, his Handmaid; hail, his Mother; and hail, all holy virtues, who, by the grace and inspiration of the Holy Spirit, are poured into the hearts of the faithful, so that, faithless no longer, they may be made servants of God through you. (*W*. 135–6)

The humility, simplicity and obedience of the Virgin was a source of endless admiration in Francis's heart.

He embraced the Mother of our Lord Jesus [wrote St Bonaventura] with indescribable love because, as he said, it was she who made the Lord of Majesty our brother, and through her we found mercy. After Christ, he put all his trust in her and took her as his patroness for himself and his friars. In her honour he fasted every year from the feast of Saints Peter and Paul until the Assumption. (*Bon.* ix, 3)

But, over and over again, he was moved by the thought of her poverty. Francis was convinced (though it is a little difficult to know on what evidence) that the Holy Family were desperately poor, and, on this account, to be greatly honoured.

Once during a meal a certain brother remarked that the Blessed Virgin was so poor that she had hardly anything to set before her Son our Lord. On hearing this, Francis sighed, deeply moved, and, leaving the table, he ate his bread sitting upon the floor. (*3 Soc.* 15)

Francis realised that the life of Christ, from his birth at Bethlehem onwards, was surrounded by danger and suffering; and he wished, so far as it was possible, to share in these sorrows and hardships. He would never accept a life of even the most modest ease and comfort knowing that 'the Son of Man had not where to lay his head'. He would be ashamed to look for respect and security when his Master had been 'despised and rejected of men'. He would think himself totally unworthy of his calling if he did not long for martyrdom when his Lord had 'set his face to go to Jerusalem', knowing full well what would happen to him there.

Francis wanted to imitate Christ in all things, especially in laying down his life for his friends. The desire for martyrdom was with him all through his life as the fitting climax to a ministry of total self-offering. The sense of commitment and of urgency runs all through the narratives. 'Burning intensely with the desire for holy martyrdom', we are told, Francis set out to go to Syria to preach the Christian faith to the Saracens. 'He was', we are told, 'carried along by so great a desire that, at times, he left behind his companion on the trip and hurried to accomplish his purpose, drunk as it were in spirit.' (*1 Cel.* 55–6) To give his life, 'to offer himself to God as a living victim by the sword of martyrdom' would be his way of 'repaying Christ for his love in dying for us and inspiring others to love God', (*Bon.* ix, 5) It was only through suffering that he could be fully 'transformed into Christ'.

It was, then, the passion of Christ which formed the basis of Francis's thought. This began on the day when the painted figure of Christ on the cross spoke to him in the church of San Damiano, and it continued for the whole of his life.

From that hour [say the Three Companions] his heart was stricken and wounded with melting love and compassion for the passion of Christ; and, for the rest of his life, he carried in it the wounds of the Lord Jesus. (*3 Soc.* 14)

Shortly afterwards we are told that he was found

roaming about alone near the church of St Mary of the Angels, weeping and lamenting aloud. A certain God-fearing man heard him and, thinking he must be ill, asked pityingly the reason for his distress. Francis replied: 'I weep for the passion of our Lord Jesus Christ; and I should not be ashamed to go weeping through the whole world for his sake'. (*3 Soc.* 14)

34

Francis was very quickly moved to tears by the thought of Christ's death upon the cross. Outward symbols, like a couple of twigs in a hedge, would immediately remind him of the cross and reduce him to tears.

Sometimes [we are told] he would pick up a stick from the ground, and laying it on his left arm, he would draw another stick across it with his right hand like a bow, as though he were playing a viol or some other instrument; and he would imitate the movements of a musician and sing in French of our Lord Jesus Christ.

Then he would see the position of the two sticks in the form of a cross and

all this jollity would end in tears, and his joy would melt away in compassion for the sufferings of Christ. And at such times he would break into constant sighs, and in his grief would forget what he was holding in his hands and be caught up in spirit into heaven. (*S.P.* 93)

On another occasion we are told that he was found 'weeping aloud over the passion of Christ as if he were seeing it with his own eyes'. (First Consideration on the Stigmata). Nor did he allow his friars for one moment to forget the passion.

Christ's cross [says Bonaventura] was their book; and they studied it day and night at the exhortation, and after the example, of their father who never stopped talking to them about the cross. (*Bon.* iv, 3)

Francis's absorption in the passion of Christ was so great that it made him almost totally indifferent to his own sufferings. Christ had done so much for him that he always felt that he ought to have done, and endured, more for Christ.

> So fervent were the love and compassion of blessed Francis for the sufferings and sorrows of Christ, and so deep was his inward and outward grief over the passion of Christ day by day that he never considered his own infirmities. (*S.P.* 91)

And yet, as we know, these were very great.

At some stage in his life Francis wrote an 'Office of the Passion' which he used to say regularly with his friars. This consists of seven Hour Services for each day, from Compline to Vespers. There are five sets, drawn up in such a way as to cover practically the whole year. Each office consists of psalms interspersed with an antiphon addressed to Our Lady. There are no readings from the Bible, and no collects, though we are told that when Francis used this office he always began with the Lord's Prayer and the Sanctus. The important thing, therefore, is the use of the psalms. Although two psalms are quoted in full (13 and 70) each of the others is what is called a 'cento' or collection of verses chosen from the Psalter as a whole. For this he draws on thirty-six psalms, the one most frequently used being Psalm 96. This is interesting because this particular psalm has no allusions to the passion. It is, in fact, a song of praise, calling upon the whole earth to worship God, rather like the *Canticle of the Sun*. The second most frequently used is Psalm 22, which is the great psalm of the passion, beginning with Christ's great cry from the cross: 'My God, my God, look upon me; why hast thou forsaken me?' In a sense these two psalms sum up what Francis was trying to do: to remind people of the indescribable sufferings of Christ on the cross and to encourage the whole of creation to give praise and glory to God for his great love.

Francis's meditations on the cross, his desire to conform to the life of Christ in every possible way and to share in his sufferings, reached their climax on La Verna, the mountain-top in the Apennines given to the saint by Orlando of Chiusi. Francis was, at the time, very much in need of a place to which he, and others of the friars, could retreat from time to time, a place where they could be sure of the privacy which they required. Francis had been told that it was the will of God that he should follow the active rather than the contemplative way, the way of service to man; but he still needed times of peaceful meditation if he was to fulfil what he knew to be his special calling.

It was in August 1224 that Francis, with a few companions went to La Verna – a somewhat inhospitable, rocky, wooded plateau – in order to meditate in depth on the sufferings of Christ. This was to cover a period of some six weeks from the Feast of the Assumption to Michaelmas; and for most of this time Francis was entirely alone on a solitary rock which could be reached only by a footbridge which the friars had made.

For the first few weeks of his retreat Francis thought over and over again about Christ's sufferings, longing in some way or other to be allowed to share in them. He had always wanted his life to be a complete and faithful imitation of the life of Christ, and he had hoped that it would end by his being martyred by the enemies of the cross. It was fairly clear now that this was not to be. He had made at least three attempts to reach the infidel, but each time his life had been spared. Although he was now only forty-two years of age he was worn down with such illness and weakness that he knew that he had not very long to live. Was there, he wondered, any way in which he could actually feel in his own body some of the pains which Christ bore on the cross?

On the feast day of the Holy Cross [14 September] Francis, sometime before dawn, began to pray outside

the entrance of his cell, turning his face to the east.
And he prayed in this way: 'My Lord, Jesus Christ, I
pray you to grant me two graces before I die: the first
is that during my life I may feel in my soul and in my
body, as much as possible, the pain which you, dear
Jesus, sustained in the hour of your most bitter passion. The second is that I may feel in my heart, as
much as possible, that excessive love with which you,
O Son of God, were inflamed in willingly enduring
such suffering for us sinners'. And remaining for a
long time in that prayer, he understood that God
would grant it to him, and that it would soon be con-
ceded to him to feel those things as much as is possible
for a mere creature. Having received this promise, St
Francis began to contemplate with intense devotion
the Passion of Christ and his infinite charity. And the
fervour of his devotion increased so much within him
that he utterly transformed himself into Jesus through
love and compassion. (Third Consideration on the
Stigmata)

Then, after a vision of an angel who 'had the likeness
of a crucified man' he knew that his prayer was to be
miraculously and mysteriously answered, and that he
was to be transformed into the likeness of Christ crucified. The narrative continues:

For soon there began to appear in the hands and feet
of St Francis the marks of nails such as he had just
seen in the body of Jesus crucified.

Francis lived for another two years after this, but
always in great pain. In an attempt to hide the Stigmata,
even from his closest friends, the wounds were never
properly attended to. The bandages which covered them
were changed each day, and this brought a little ease;
but, very typically, Francis refused to have them changed

on a Friday because 'for the love of Christ, on the day of the crucifixion he wished to hang, truly crucified with Christ in the sufferings of the cross'.

Francis was not martyred in the usual sense of the term, though he must have come very near to it when he walked out into no-man's land which lay between the embattled armies in Egypt; nor did he die of hunger and exposure, though there were times, especially in the early days, when the friars came very near to starvation. God reserved for him a special form of suffering which brought him very close to his crucified Lord. For two years he was in continuous, and sometimes agonising, pain as he lived, often in damp caves and filthy leper-houses, with five open wounds in his hands and feet and side. In addition to this he suffered from blindness, dropsy, and terrible stomach ulcers. Yet in all this he was full of joy because he knew that, however great might be his pain, it was never to be compared with the pain that Jesus had suffered on our behalf.

As time went on his pains grew worse. Celano takes up the narrative:

> As his infirmity increased, all his bodily strength failed; and, destitute of all his powers, he could not move himself at all. Still, when he was asked by a certain brother what he would prefer to bear, this lingering and long illness or the suffering of a severe martyrdom at the hands of an executioner, he replied: 'My son, that has always been and still is most dear to me and more sweet and more acceptable which pleases the Lord my God most to let happen in me and with me, for I desire always only to be found conformed and obedient to his will in all things. Yet, this infirmity is harder for me to bear even for three days than any martyrdom. I am not speaking of the reward, but only of the intensity of suffering it causes'. (*1 Cel.* 107)

This intense suffering was a kind of martyrdom, a lingering death brought on by the hardships which he had so willingly accepted in his determination to follow, in every detail, the teaching of the Master whom he so dearly loved.

The Holy Spirit

When Francis was twenty years old there died, in the far south of Italy, the prophet called Joachim of Fiore, whose writings were to have a considerable influence upon the Church in later years, not least among some of those who owed their inspiration and their loyalty to St Francis. Joachim had divided up the history of the world on a Trinitarian basis, the first period being the Age of the Father, covering the years from Creation to the birth of Christ. The second period, the Age of the Son, began with the Nativity and continued down to about the year 1200 during which the Church, as the Body of Christ, had continued his work. This was to be superseded by the Age of the Spirit which was about to be inaugurated by the appearance of new kinds of religious orders, as a result of whose example and teaching great changes would take place in the life of the Church which would now become less organised and hierocratic and consequently more spiritual.

It is extremely unlikely that Francis had ever heard of Joachim, and even more unlikely that he had ever read any of his works. Francis was not really interested in that kind of prophesying with its theological basis and its wide vistas. But he would have welcomed the call to a new kind of Christian life in which the Holy Spirit would take control of man and lead him to higher levels of devotion and service. Francis did not, in fact, talk much about the Holy Spirit, though he was always very much aware of his presence and of his activity. To Francis, God the Father was the creator and originator of all things, the fount of love and the object of all praise and devotion. Similarly God the Son was the teacher and pattern, who gave us the example of the life of perfect obedience to the will of the Father. So it might be said that God the Holy Spirit was the personification of the love which passed between the Father and the Son, the Interpreter of the Word, the Advocate and Comforter by whose wisdom and power man was able to enter into the fulness of God's love and enjoy the blessedness of redemption.

When Francis refers to the Holy Spirit it is mostly in conventional phrases such as an ascription to the Trinity or the rounding off of a prayer. But he fully understood the 'personality' of the Spirit whom, at one point, he declared to be the true Minister General of the Order (*2 Cel.* 193), while, in his last injunctions to St Clare, he begged her and her sisters to 'espouse themselves to the Holy Spirit.' (*W.* 76).

So far as his own life was concerned, Francis might well have used a verse from Psalm 31 to express his dependence upon God the Holy Spirit. 'Thou art my rock and my fortress,' says the psalmist, 'for thy name's sake lead me also and guide me.' Francis certainly saw the Holy Spirit as both a fortress and a guide. In the very difficult and demanding life which he had chosen he needed a place of refuge, somewhere to which he could go for the wisdom and strength which he knew the Holy Spirit of God would provide for him.

Francis [we are told] learned in his prayer that the presence of the Holy Spirit for which he longed was granted more intimately when he was far from the rush of worldly affairs. Therefore, he used to seek out lonely places in the wilderness and go into abandoned churches to pray at night;

41

and Bonaventura goes on to describe a fearful hand-to-hand fight with the devil which Francis won only by means of the strength which God supplied through his Holy Spirit. (*Bon.* x, 3). Or again:

> Francis would never let any call of the Spirit go unanswered. When he experienced it he would make the most of it and enjoy the consolation afforded him in this way for so long as God permitted it. If he was on a journey, and felt the near approach of God's Spirit, he would stop and let his companions go on while he drank in the joy of this new inspiration. He refused to offer God's grace an ineffectual welcome. He was often taken right out of himself in a rapture of contemplation, so that he was lost in ecstasy and had no idea what was going on about him, while he experienced things which were beyond all human understanding. (*Bon.* x, 2)

If Francis found the Spirit his 'rock and his fortress' he made him also his 'leader and his guide'. There were a great many occasions in his life when guidance was needed. From the time of his 'conversion' right through to the end, Francis knew that he was being guided, step by step, by the Holy Spirit whom he depended upon as interpreter of the will of the Father and of the demands of the Son. He knew that it was only by the power of the Spirit that he had had the courage to go forward into the unseen and unknown, and to accept the risks involved in such things as getting rid of all his possessions, of refusing to touch money, of living with lepers, or setting out to walk across the battlefields and into the tent of the Soldan.

Francis was very conscious of the Holy Spirit at his shoulder at all times to tell him what to say and what to do. This comes out particularly in his preaching which he always regarded as the most important of his activities. At the very beginning of his ministry, when he had accepted the call to renunciation and poverty, he set out to tell people about God and to inspire them to penitence.

> Divinely inspired, he began to speak in public very simply of penitence and the life of evangelical perfection. His words were not treated with ridicule, neither were they spoken in vain; for they possessed the strength of the Holy Spirit and went straight to the hearts of the listeners rousing them to vehement astonishment. (*3 Soc.* 25)

As time went on, vast crowds came to hear him preach. Francis fully realised the responsibility which this involved, and, on such occasions, we are told that he learned to depend entirely upon the guidance which he knew would be given to him. Celano tells us that

> when he so very often preached the word of God to thousands of people, he was as sure of himself as though he were speaking with a familiar companion. He looked upon the greatest multitude of people as one person, and he preached to one as he would to a multitude. Out of the purity of his mind he provided for himself security in preaching a sermon, and, without thinking about it beforehand, he spoke wonderful things to all and things not heard before. When he did give some time to meditation before a sermon, he at times forgot what he had meditated upon when the people had come together, and he knew nothing else to say. Without embarrassment he would confess to the people that he had thought of many things but could remember nothing at all of them; and suddenly he would be filled with such great eloquence that he would move the souls of the hearers to admiration. At times, however, knowing nothing to

43

say, he would give a blessing and dismiss the people,
feeling that from this alone they had received a great
sermon. (*1 Cel.* 72)

The most striking instance of his reliance on the inspiration of the Holy Spirit was when he had the rather
unexpected privilege of preaching before the pope and
the cardinals.

When St Francis was due to preach before Pope
Honorius, he had his sermon all prepared on the advice of [the Bishop of Ostia afterwards Pope] Gregory;
but when he began to speak he could not remember a
word. Then he told them: 'Someone wrote a sermon
for me, and it was a profound sermon which I was to
preach to you. But now I have forgotten all of it. If you
will wait a little while I shall pray to God and he will
give me something to say'. Then he gave himself to
prayer, and he preached a marvellous sermon. (*Bon.
Opera Omnia,* ix, 579)

Bonaventura stops at this point; but Celano, from
whom the story comes, adds certain details which
Bonaventura perhaps thought it better not to mention.

He spoke with such fervour of spirit [says Celano]
that, not being able to contain himself for joy, when he
spoke the words with his mouth, he moved his feet as
though he were dancing, not indeed lustfully, but as
one burning with the fire of divine love, not provoking
laughter but drawing forth tears of grief. For many of
them were pierced to the heart in admiration of divine
grace and of such constancy in man. But the venerable
Lord Bishop of Ostia was kept in suspense by fear,
and he prayed with all his strength to the Lord that
the simplicity of the blessed man would not be despised, since the glory of the saint would reflect upon

himself as would his disgrace, inasmuch as he had been placed over Francis's family as a father. (*1 Cel.* 73)

There is no doubt of Francis's constant realisation of the presence and guidance of the Holy Spirit, and of the strength and courage which was given to him. Life for him was very hard, very dangerous, very exacting. He was deeply conscious of his responsibility to those who had given up so much to follow him, and he used often to say that 'it behoved him to be a model and an example for all the brethren'. His standards were so high that he knew that he would never reach them unless he learned to depend, at all times, on divine grace. As Celano writes:

Therefore the blessed Francis was being daily filled with the consolation and the grace of the Holy Spirit; and with all vigilance and solicitude he was forming his new sons with new learning, teaching them to walk with undeviating steps the way of holy poverty and blessed simplicity. One day, when he was wondering over the mercy of the Lord with regard to the gifts bestowed upon him, he wished that the course of his own life and that of his brothers might be shown him by the Lord, he sought out a place of prayer, as he had done so often, and he persevered there for a long time with fear and trembling standing before the Lord of the whole earth, and he thought in the bitterness of his soul of the years he had spent wretchedly, frequently repeating these words: 'God, be merciful to me, a sinner'. Little by little a certain unspeakable joy and very great sweetness began to flood his innermost heart. He began also to stand aloof from himself, and, as his feelings were checked, and the darkness that had gathered in his heart because of his fear of sin dispelled, there was poured into him a certainty that all his sins had been forgiven, and a confidence of his restoration was given him. He was then caught up above himself and absorbed in a certain light; the capacity of his mind was enlarged, and he could see clearly what was to come to pass. When this sweetness finally passed, along with the light, renewed in spirit he seemed changed into another man. (*1 Cel.* 26)

Francis expressed all this in the prayer with which he concluded his letter to the friars meeting together in Chapter:

Almighty, eternal, just and merciful God, grant us in our misery that we may do, for thy sake alone, what we know thou dost want us to do, and that we may always want what pleases thee; so that, cleansed and inwardly enlightened and fired with the ardour of the Holy Spirit, we may be able to follow in the footsteps of thy Son, our Lord Jesus Christ, and so make our way to thee, Most High, by thy grace alone, who livest and reignest in perfect Trinity and simple Unity, and art glorified, God all-powerful, for ever and ever. Amen. (*W.* 108)

3. FRANCIS AND THE CHURCH

The Church

By the time when St Francis had brought together a band of disciples and so laid the foundation not only of a new religious Order but of a new type of religious, there was a good deal of dissatisfaction and unrest among churchpeople, and talk of the need for reform. People complained that the Church was too centralised, too authoritarian, too rich and too powerful, and that it was not giving to the general public the spiritual help which they needed.

There were very large numbers of clergy about the place, but many of the abler men were enticed or ordered into the service of the State or of the law and so were unable to attend to the needs of the people whom they were intended to serve. Many of the richer clergy, especially those connected with the ruling families, were pluralists on the grand scale, rectors of many parishes and rarely seen in any of them. Of the clergy who actually lived among the people, many were ill educated and some were idle. They mostly had a hard struggle to live on the very low incomes which they managed to get, and they often became involved in disputes with their parishioners over things like the payment of tithes. There were, of course, many good and faithful priests, like Chaucer's

47

'poor parson' of a later age; but the standards of the parochial clergy around the year 1200 were not very high.

Meanwhile the monastic Orders, which attracted a large number of men, were, by their very nature, cut off from the people. Isolated and secure in their vast abbeys, often independent of episcopal jurisdiction and interference, the monks occupied themselves either with literary work or with the management of their large estates and households and took little interest in the affairs of the laity who were not really their concern.

This feeling of being neglected and ill served had led to the creation of a number of sects whose members were very critical of the Church, which they tended to regard as beyond reform. Their only hope was to cut themselves off from the Church and start something of their own. Groups like the Cathari and the Waldenses were attracting people by the radicalism of their teaching and the hope of better things. They told people not to obey bishops and priests, not to pay their tithes, not to attend the services of the Church or receive the sacraments. All these things, they said, were acting against the will of God by drawing people away from the simple teaching of the Gospel.

Francis was just as much aware of the need for reform and renewal as were any of the heretics. He knew that people wanted to hear the word of God, and that the poor were often neglected. But never for one moment did he think of setting up something which would want to act against the authority of the Church. His doctrines of humility and obedience, as essential to all Christian behaviour, made this impossible. To him the Church was everything. It was the instrument through which God's work was done and no good work could be done without it. So when the number of his disciples had risen to twelve, the first thing he did was to set off for Rome in the hope of arousing the interest of the Pope in what they were trying to do, and of receiving his blessing on their mission to the world.

Blessed Francis said: 'I will go and entrust the Order of Friars Minor to the holy Roman Church. The rod of her authority will daunt and restrain those who wish it ill, and the sons of God will everywhere enjoy full freedom to pursue their eternal salvation. Let her sons acknowledge the kindly blessings of their Mother, and embrace her sacred feet with particular devotion.

'Under her protection no harm will come upon the Order, and the son of Satan will not trample over the vineyard of the Lord with impunity. Our holy Mother will herself imitate the glory of our poverty, and will not permit our observance of humility to be overshadowed by the cloud of pride. She will preserve unimpaired the bonds of love and peace that exist between us, and will impose her gravest censure on the unruly. The sacred observance of evangelical poverty will ever flourish before her, and she will never allow the fragrance of our good name and holy life to be destroyed.' (*S.P.* 78)

Francis wanted, if possible, to work in collaboration with the parish clergy, since he and they were trying to do the same thing.

Blessed Francis [says the *Mirror of Perfection*] wished his sons to be at peace with all men and to behave themselves humbly to everyone; but he showed them by his own words and example to be especially humble to the clergy. For he said: 'We have been sent to help the clergy in the salvation of souls, so that we may supply whatever is lacking in them. But men will not be rewarded according to their office, but their work. Remember, my brothers, that the winning of souls is what pleases God most, and we can do this better by

working in harmony with the clergy than in opposition'. (*S.P.* 54)

It would have been very easy for some of his followers
to become critical of the clergy, for their faults and in-
adequacies were obvious; but this Francis would never
allow. Because God had called and ordained a man to
the priesthood, and had given him power to turn the
bread and wine into the Body and Blood of Christ, a
priest was a man to be respected even if his private life
was dissolute. As Francis wrote in his *Testament*:

God inspired me, and still inspires me with such great
faith in priests who live according to the laws of the
holy Church of Rome, because of their dignity, that if
they persecuted me I should still be ready to turn to
them for aid. And if I were as wise as Solomon and
met the poorest priests of the world, I would still
refuse to preach against their will in the parishes in
which they live. I am determined to reverence, love
and honour priests and all others as my superiors. I
refuse to consider their sins because I can see the Son
of God in them, and they are better than I. I do this
because in this world I cannot see the most high Son of
God with my own eyes, except for his most holy Body
and Blood which they receive and they alone ad-
minister to others. (*W.* 67)

Again, he wrote, in an Admonition to the friars:

Blessed is that servant of God who has confidence in
priests who live according to the laws of the holy
Roman Church. Woe to those who despise them. Even
if they fall into sin, no one should pass judgement on
them, for God has reserved judgement on them to
himself. They are in a privileged position because they
have charge of the Body and Blood of our Lord Jesus

50

Christ, which they receive and which they alone ad-
minister to others; and so anyone who sins against
them commits a greater crime than if he sinned
against anyone else in the whole world. (*W*. 86)

or, in the 'Letter to the General Chapter':

Listen to this, my brothers: If it is right to honour the
Blessed Virgin Mary because she bore him in her most
holy womb; if St John the Baptist trembled and was
afraid even to touch Christ's sacred head; if the tomb
where he lay for only a short time is so venerated; how
holy, and virtuous, and worthy should not a priest be.
He touches Christ with his own hands, Christ who is
to die now no more but enjoy eternal life and glory,
upon whom the angels desire to look. (*W*. 105)

All this is very different from the sort of thing which
was being said by those who wished to draw people away
from their allegiance to the Church. Francis never tired
of impressing upon people the importance of showing
respect to the priests. And this he did to prevent any
possible risk of his community being regarded as in any
way opposed to the established hierarchy and the appointed ministry of the Church.

Francis also had a great love for church buildings. We
are told that, in the very early days of his conversion, he
loved to buy vases and other objects pertaining to the service and adornment of churches, and to send them
secretly to poor priests. We know also that, after the vision in the church of San Damiano he worked for some
time repairing ruined churches. Later we read of him going about with a broom to sweep out churches which
were dirty because he always felt sad when he found any
church neglected or uncared for. A church was to him a
place where God was always to be found, and his heart
was uplifted whenever he saw one.

If a church were standing in any place whatsoever [wrote Celano] even though the brothers were not present there but could see it only from a distance, they were to prostrate themselves upon the ground in its direction and, having bowed low with body and soul, they were to adore Almighty God, saying: 'We adore thee, Christ, here and in all thy churches' as the holy father had taught them. And, what is no less to be admired, wherever they saw a crucifix or the mark of a cross, whether upon the ground, or upon a wall, or on trees, or in the hedges along the way, they were to do the same thing. (*1 Cel.* 45)

The Bible

It is not always realised how greatly the medieval man loved and respected the Bible. Of course he did not read it regularly, as people have done in later generations, partly because the common man could not read at all, and partly because Bibles, having always to be written out by hand, were extremely expensive. But those who possessed or had access to Bibles often knew them extraordinarily well. In the published sermons of the great fifteenth-century Franciscan preacher, Bernardino of Siena, there are quoted nearly 4,000 different texts from the Old Testament and 2,600 from the New.

St Bonaventura tells us that St Francis 'had never studied Sacred Scripture' (*Bon.* xi, 1); but, if this is true, he certainly became well acquainted with it in later life. We have only to look at the Offices which he compiled to see how his mind was steeped in the Scriptures. Or again, in the six letters which he wrote, which now cover fifteen pages of print, we find no less than fifty-three texts from the Bible – fifteen from the Old Testament and thirty-eight from the New. When he came to write the

Primitive Rule in 1209, the one which he proposed to present to the Pope as a pattern of how he and his followers intended to live, he wrote it, as Thomas of Celano says, 'simply and in a few words, using mainly the precepts of the holy Gospels, to whose perfection he earnestly aspired' (*1 Cel.* 32). Because this was so, the Rule was extremely demanding; and it was, perhaps, not surprising that Innocent III, who was naturally suspicious of new communities being formed, thought that this little band of itinerant evangelists were setting their standards too high, and was very reluctant to give them his approval. He would probably have sent them away empty-handed had not one of the cardinals said: 'We must be careful. If we refuse this beggarman's request because it is new or too difficult, we may be sinning against Christ's Gospel, because he is only asking us to approve a form of Gospel life. Anyone who says that a vow to live according to the perfection of the Gospel contains something new or unreasonable or too difficult to be observed, is guilty of blasphemy against Christ, the Author of the Gospel'. (*Bon.* iii, 9)

Francis's whole way of life was based on the teaching of Jesus which he wished to observe in every detail. It was, therefore, to the Gospels that he turned again and again when he needed guidance. When the opulent and distinguished Bernard of Quintavalle suddenly declared that he wished to follow Francis in a life of poverty and humility, the saint rushed to the Bible for help. He took Bernard along to a church in Assisi, where, after earnest prayer, they solemnly opened at random the Gospel book on the altar only to find written: 'If you will be perfect, go, sell what you have and give to the poor'. A second and third opening gave two further texts: 'Take nothing for your journey' and 'If any man will come after me let him deny himself'. Francis was so certain that he could hear God speaking to him personally through the Scriptures that he used this method of communicating with him on several occasions. Once, towards the end of his life, when he was passing through a time of great anxiety and suffering, he again sought God's help and advice.

By divine inspiration [wrote Bonaventura] he learned that if he opened the Gospels, Christ would reveal to him what was God's will for him and what God wished to see realised in him. And so Francis prayed fervently and took the Gospel book from the altar, telling his companion, a devout and holy friar, to open it in the name of the Blessed Trinity. He opened the Gospel three times, and each time it opened at the Passion, and so Francis understood that he must become like Christ in the distress and agony of his Passion before he left the world, just as he had been like him in all that he did during his life. (*Bon.* xiii, 2)

It was because Francis had such reverence for the Scriptures that he always wanted to treat Bibles with the greatest possible respect. In a letter to the friars he wrote:

I urge all my friars and I encourage them in Christ to show all possible respect for God's words wherever they may happen to find them in writing. If they are not kept properly, or if they lie thrown about disrespectfully, they should pick them up and put them aside, paying honour in his words to God who spoke them. God's words sanctify numerous objects, and it is by the power of the words of Christ that the sacrament of the altar is consecrated. (*W.* 107)

Celano tells us that

He was filled with love that passes all human understanding when he pronounced your holy name, O holy Lord; and, carried away with joy and purest gladness, he seemed like a new man, one from another

54

world. Therefore, whenever he would find anything written, whether about God or about man, along the way, or in a house, or on the floor, he would pick it up with the greatest reverence and put it in a sacred or decent place, so that the name of the Lord would not remain there or anything else pertaining to it. One day when he was asked by a certain brother why he so diligently picked up writings even of pagans, or writings in which there was no mention of the name of the Lord, he replied: 'Son, because the letters are there out of which the most glorious name of the Lord God could be put together. Whatever is good there does not pertain to the pagans, nor to any other men, but to God alone, to whom belongs all good'. (*1 Cel.* 82)

Francis, then, taught his friars to treat the Bible with great reverence since it was the word of God and the book of rules which they were bound to obey. Poverty made it impossible for them to own Bibles, but they clearly had the use of them, though charity sometimes induced them to part with what they regarded as their most cherished possession. Once they were given a New Testament which they used for saying the Offices; but when a poor woman came begging for alms for the love of God, Francis told Brother Peter that, as they had nothing else to give, they must give her the book. 'Give the New Testament to our mother', he said, 'so that she can sell it for her needs. I am sure that this will please our Lord and the Blessed Virgin better than if we were to read from it.' (*S.P.* 38)

Francis himself was often praised for his wisdom in interpreting the Scriptures. The *Mirror of Perfection* tells us that

while he was staying in Siena he was visited by a Doctor of Theology from the Order of Preachers, a man who was both humble and sincerely spiritual. When he had discussed the words of our Lord with blessed Francis for some time, this doctor asked him about the passage in Ezekiel: 'When I threaten the sinner with doom of death, it is for thee to give him word and warn him'. And he said: 'Good father, I know many people who are in mortal sin, and do not warn them of their wickedness. Will their souls be required at my hand?' Blessed Francis humbly answered that he was no scholar, so that it would be more profitable for him to receive instruction from his questioner than to offer his own opinion on Scripture. The humble doctor then added: 'Brother, although I have heard this passage expounded by various learned men, I would be glad to know how you interpret it'. So blessed Francis said: 'If the passage is to be understood in general terms, I take it to mean that a servant of God should burn and shine in such a way by his own life and holiness that he rebukes all wicked people by the light of his example and the devoutness of his conversation. In this way the brightness of his life and the fragrance of his reputation will make all men aware of their own wickedness'. Greatly edified, the doctor went away, and said to the companions of blessed Francis: 'My brothers, this man's theology is grounded on purity and contemplation, and resembles a flying eagle while our knowledge crawls along the ground on its belly'. (*S.P.* 53)

Francis's reply to the learned Dominican reveals his conviction that preaching to sinners was not likely to do much good by itself. What would impress (and warn) them was to see a man living a life of holiness and self-discipline. This is typical of Francis's attitude towards the Bible: it was always there to teach people about God and to encourage them to live as God would have them live. It was for this reason that he was very suspicious of those who boasted of their knowledge, and very hard on friars who wanted to possess books in order to become more learned. In one of his *Admonitions* to the friars Francis said:

> St Paul tells us that 'The letter kills, but the spirit gives life'. A man has been killed by the letter when he wants to know quotations only so that people will think he is very learned and he can make money to give to his relatives and friends. A religious has been killed by the letter when he has no desire to follow the spirit of Sacred Scripture, but wants to know what it says only so that he can explain it to others. On the other hand, those have received life from the spirit of Sacred Scripture who, by their words and example, refer to the most high God, to whom belongs all good, all that they know or wish to know, and do not allow their knowledge to become a source of self-complacency. (*W.* 81)

Nevertheless, he wanted his brethren to read and study the Bible as much as was possible, so long as they did not sin against the principles of poverty and humility. As Bonaventura tells us in one of his letters:

> In order that you may know how much St Francis approved of Bible-reading, let me tell you what I heard from a certain friar. He told me that when a copy of the New Testament was given to the brethren, and since it was impossible for them all to read it at once, St Francis divided it up into single sheets and gave one page to each brother, in order that all might study it and none interfere with another. (*N.F.* 48)

Not, perhaps, a very intelligent way to read the Bible; but Francis would have no doubt that, by this means, God would convey some precious message to his erring children.

The Eucharist

Francis's devotion to Christ was, as we know, the very centre of his life. He had set out to follow Christ and to obey each one of his commands, however costly this might be. In many ways he felt as close to his Master as the first disciples had felt. Everything that Jesus had said and done was familiar to him, made so by his constant meditation on the Gospels. He felt particularly close to Christ in everything that was connected with his sufferings, and he prayed that he might share in them (so far as such a thing was humanly possible) and was rewarded by the long agony of the Stigmata.

Francis's passion to be with Christ in all that he did, and in the life which he had chosen to live, gave him a special devotion to the Eucharist, which he saw as a unique meeting-place with Christ where he came as near as it was possible to see and to touch him. Jesus had told his disciples that the bread and wine of the Eucharist were, in fact, his Body and his Blood, his physical being; and Francis had taken this literally. That was why he was so insistent that people should show respect for the priests, and especially to their hands, since it was they who made possible this physical contact with the Risen Christ.

Francis [said Celano] burned with a love that came from his whole being for the sacrament of the Lord's Body, and he was carried away with wonder at the loving condescension and the most condescending love shown there. Not to hear at least one Mass each day, if he could be there, he considered no small contempt. He frequently received Holy Communion, and he did so with such devotion that he made others also devout. (*2 Cel.* 201)

It was in one of his *Admonitions* to the friars that he worked out the theology of his devotion to the Eucharist.

Sacred Scripture [he wrote] tells us that the Father dwells in light inaccessible and that God is spirit; and St John adds that no one at any time has seen God. Because God is a spirit he can be seen only in spirit: it is the spirit that gives life; the flesh profits nothing. But God the Son is equal to the Father, and so he too can be seen only in the same way as the Father and the Holy Spirit. That is why all those were condemned who saw our Lord, Jesus Christ, in his humanity but did not see or believe in spirit in his divinity, that he was the true Son of God. In the same way now, all those are condemned who see the sacrament of the Body of Christ which is consecrated on the altar in the form of bread and wine by the words of our Lord in the hands of the priest, and do not see or believe in spirit and in God that this is really the most holy Body and Blood of our Lord, Jesus Christ. (*W*. 78)

And he went on to say:

Every day Jesus humbles himself just as he did when he came from his heavenly throne into the Virgin's womb; every day he comes to us and lets us see him in abjection, when he descends from the bosom of the Father into the hands of the priest at the altar. He shows himself to us in this sacred bread just as he once appeared to his apostles in real flesh. With their own eyes they saw only his flesh, but they believed that he was God, because they contemplated him with the eyes of the spirit. We too, with our own eyes, see only bread and wine; but we must see further and firmly believe that this is his most holy Body and Blood, living and true. (ibid.)

In the early days the Franciscan brotherhood was a community of laymen. But it was not long before the Order attracted men who were in priest's orders, with whom Francis pleaded that they should never forget how great was the honour and privilege which had been bestowed upon them. Writing in later years to the priest friars, he poured out his concern that they should treat the Sacrament with the greatest possible respect:

Kissing your feet with all the love that I am capable of [he wrote], I beg you to show the greatest possible reverence and honour for the most holy Body and Blood of our Lord Jesus Christ, through whom all things, whether on earth or in heaven, have been brought to peace and reconciled with Almighty God. And I implore all my friars who are priests now or who will be priests in the future, all those who want to be priests of the Most High, to be free from all earthly affection when they say Mass, and offer single-mindedly and with reverence the true sacrifice of the most holy Body and Blood of our Lord Jesus Christ with a holy and pure intention, not for any earthly gain or through human respect or love for any human being, not serving to the eye as pleasers of men. With the help of God's grace, their whole attention should be fixed on him, with a will to please the most high Lord alone, because it is he alone who accomplished this marvel in his own way. (*W*. 104)

And to the friars as a whole he wrote:

Our whole being should be seized with fear, the whole world should tremble and heaven rejoice, when Christ the Son of the living God is present on the altar in the hands of the priest. What wonderful majesty! What stupendous condescension! O sublime humility! O humble sublimity! That the Lord of the whole universe, God and the Son of God, should humble himself like this and hide under the form of a little bread for our salvation. (ibid.)

4. THE FOUR FOUNDATION-STONES

Francis was convinced that to be a Christian was to be like Christ, and that to be a perfect Christian was to follow Christ in every possible way. Christianity was, as he knew well, a faith, a matter of belief. No one could call himself a Christian unless he were wholly committed to belief in God – Father, Son and Holy Spirit. We have already looked at the faith of St Francis: what it meant to him to believe in God. But Francis was also convinced that if you believe in God in this sort of way, then your life must be a reflection of your faith. It was Francis's greatest desire to stir up in people a firmer belief in God; but he realised that this was not going to be done just by preaching moving sermons and uttering powerful admonitions. He knew well enough that people were far more likely to be roused by example than by words; and that was why he set out to show, as far as it was possible, what the full Christian life really meant.

Francis knew that God did not expect all his children to live the same sort of life. Human life is complex and multifarious, and each man has his own vocation. Some, he believed, were called to voluntary poverty; but this was not the only way to fulfil one's vocation, or civilisation could not go on. Some were called to forgo the joys of family life; but this could not apply to all, or life would come to an end. Some might even be called to martyrdom; but this was obviously a very specialised form of service and self-sacrifice which only very few could make.

As the result of a series of experiences in his youth, it became clear to Francis that God had called him to a special type of Christian life, a type which would demand great courage and determination and which would carry with it great hardship and pain. The life which he chose might have ended in an early death from hunger, disease or exposure, or even, perhaps, at the hands of cruel men. This was something which Francis accepted as the price which he was willing to pay out of his treasury of love and obedience. And when other men came to him and said that they wished to go with him, he made it clear to them that the standards which he had accepted were paramount and could not be reduced or mitigated in the smallest degree. As he wrote in his *Testament*:

> When God gave me some friars there was no one to tell me what I should do; but the Most High himself made it clear to me that I must live of the Gospel. (*W* .68)

By this he meant that every recorded word of Christ was to be taken at its face value, and, if it was in the form of a command, it was to be obeyed at whatever cost. There could be no arguing with the voice of God.

So it came about when, in later years, attempts were made by some of the friars to persuade Francis to allow some concessions, especially in the field of scholarship, he laid down what he regarded as the four essentials or foundation-stones on which his ideal of the Christian life was built. As Brother Leo writes:

> The most holy father did not wish his friars to hanker after learning and books, but taught them to build their lives on holy Humility, to practise pure Simplicity and devout Prayer, and to love Lady Poverty, on which the saints and first friars had established themselves. He used to say that this was the only sure road to their salvation and the edification of others,

because Christ, whom we are called to follow, showed and taught us this way alone by his teaching and example. (*S.P.* 72)

Leo goes on:

Looking into the future, the blessed father knew through the Holy Spirit, and often told the friars, that in the hope of edifying others, many would abandon their vocation, which is holy Humility, pure Simplicity, Prayer and devotion, and the love of Lady Poverty. He said: 'Because they will think themselves more gifted, more filled with devotion, fired with love, and enlightened by divine knowledge through their study of the Scriptures, they will, as a result, remain inwardly cold and empty. Consequently, they will be unable to return to their first vocation because they will have wasted the time when they should have been following this vocation in useless and misguided study. I fear that even the grace that they seemed to possess will be taken away from them, because they have completely neglected the grace that had been given to them, which is to hold to and follow their true vocation'. (ibid.)

Francis then went on to speak of the 'holy, poor, humble and simple brethren' who were faithful to their calling.

These [he said] are my Knights of the Round Table, who remain hidden in deserts and lonely places in order to devote themselves more completely to prayer and meditation, lamenting their own sins and the sins of others, living simply and behaving humbly, whose sanctity is known to God, and at times to other friars, but unknown to the world. When the angels present their souls before God he will show them the fruit and reward of their labours, namely, the many souls that have been saved by their prayers and tears. And he will say to them: 'My dear sons, these souls have been saved by your prayers, tears and example, and since you have been faithful over little things, I have great things to commit to your charge. Other men have preached and laboured with their words of wisdom and learning, but through your merits I have brought about the fruit of salvation. So receive the reward of your labours, and the fruit of your merits, which is an everlasting kingdom gained by your humility and simplicity, and by the power of your prayers and tears'. (ibid.)

Finally, Francis declared:

> Those who have cared for nothing except to know and point out the way of salvation to others, and have made no effort to follow it themselves, will stand naked and empty-handed before the judgement-seat of Christ, bearing only the sheaves of confusion, shame and grief. Then shall the truth of holy Humility and Simplicity, of holy Prayer and Poverty, which is our vocation, be exalted, glorified and proclaimed. (ibid.)

Three times in this passage reference is made to the four qualities of Humility, Simplicity, Poverty and Prayer. It was upon these foundations that the Franciscan way of life was built.

Humility

In Francis's eyes humility had a twofold character; there was the inner humility which a man feels in his heart, and the outer humility which he shows to the world. Humility must, therefore, control your inmost thoughts and also the way in which you live your life.

Like all great saints, Francis was intensely aware of his own failings, his inability to reach the standards of perfection which he had set himself, his hidden pride, his desire sometimes to dominate, his occasional lapses in charity. No one can ever have confessed his sins with greater earnestness, begging God to pardon one whom he knew to be a sinner. Francis himself explained this to one of his friends.

When the time of the Chapter was approaching, blessed Francis said to his companion: 'It seems to me that I would not be a true Friar Minor unless I were in the state that I will describe to you. Suppose that the friars invite me to the Chapter with great respect and devotion, and, touched by their devotion, I go to the Chapter with them. During the assembly they ask me to proclaim the word of God and preach before them, so I rise and preach to them as the Holy Spirit moves me. Suppose that after my sermon they all cry out against me, saying: "We will not have you to rule over us. You have not the necessary eloquence, and you are too stupid and simple. We are very ashamed to have such a simple and contemptible Superior over us. Henceforth do not presume to call yourself our Superior". So they depose me with abuse and contempt. It seems to me that I should not be a true Friar Minor unless I were just as happy when they abused me and deposed me in disgrace, unwilling that I should remain their Superior, as when they held me in respect and honour, for in either case their welfare and usefulness is my first desire. For if I was happy when they praised and honoured me in their devotion – which may well be a danger to my soul – I ought to rejoice and be far happier at the benefit and health brought to my soul when they abuse me, for this is a sure spiritual gain'. (*S.P.* 64)

It is very unlikely that anything of this kind ever took place, as the friars had such love for Francis and such devotion to him that they would be very unlikely ever to treat him in that sort of way, or say such unkind things to him. But there was one Chapter Meeting when Francis met with considerable opposition and had to speak very sternly to the friars who, he thought, were in danger of losing their humility and simplicity.

This was what is called the 'Chapter of the Mats', at which an attempt was made to persuade Francis to abandon the very hard Rule which he had drawn up and accept one of the standard Rules of the monastic Orders, Benedictine, Augustinian or Cistercian. Only so, thought some of the brothers, could the Order of Friars Minor fit itself into the life of the Church and give the service which was needed. What, in fact, they wanted was that more opportunity should be provided for study, so that, like the followers of St Dominic, the friars could become more of a preaching Order and join in the battle against heresy which, they thought, was poisoning the life of the Church. So some of the senior members enlisted the help of Ugolino, the Cardinal Bishop of Ostia, to try to persuade Francis to withdraw his own Rule and allow them to accept something less demanding and less rigid, something which would make it possible to have at least access to books and places in which to read them.

Francis was deeply shocked. He saw that anything of this kind would undermine his most cherished beliefs. He did not want his friars to be learned preachers. All he wanted was that they should live the Christian life as he understood it in all its fulness, and thereby call people to penitence. This is the account of what happened.

> The cardinal repeated to blessed Francis all that they had said in the form of advice; but, without making any answer, he took the cardinal by the hand and led him before the brothers assembled in Chapter. And he

spoke to them in the fervour and power of the Holy Spirit, saying: 'My brothers! My brothers! God has called me by the way of simplicity and humility, and has in truth revealed this way for me and for all who are willing to trust and to follow me. So I do not want you to quote any other Rule to me, whether that of St Benedict, St Augustine or St Bernard, or to recommend any other way or form of life except this way which God, in his mercy, has revealed and given to me. The Lord told me that he wished me to be a new fool in this world, and he does not want us to live by any other wisdom but this'. (*S.P.* 68)

To be sincerely humble; to know in the depths of your being that you were a fool and a sinner; to weep for your wickedness and insufficiency; to plead daily and hourly for God's mercy; to turn all the praise and devotion of men into contrition and penitence for having so disastrously failed them – this was something essential to Francis.

The *Little Flowers* has a story of how

one day, as St Francis was returning from his prayers in the wood, at the entrance to the wood Brother Masseo met him; and, wishing to test how humble he was, asked in a mocking manner, saying: 'Why after thee? why after thee? why after thee?' St Francis replied: 'What is it thou wouldst say?' And Brother Masseo answered: 'Tell me, why is it that all the world comes after thee, and everybody desires to see thee, and to hear thee, and to obey thee? Thou art not a man either comely of person, or of noble birth, or of great knowledge. Whence then comes it that all the world runs after thee?'

Hearing this St Francis, filled with joy in his spirit, raised his face to heaven and remained for a great while with his mind lifted up to God; then, returning to himself, he knelt down and gave praise and thanks to God; and then, with great fervour of spirit, turning to Brother Masseo, he said: 'Wouldst thou know why after me? Wouldst thou know why after me? why all the world runs after me? This happens to me because the eyes of the most high God, which behold in all places both the evil and the good, even those most holy eyes have not seen amongst sinners one more vile, nor more insufficient, nor a greater sinner than I, and therefore to do that wonderful work which he intends to do he has not found on earth a viler creature than I; and for this cause he has elected me to confound the nobility and the grandeur and the strength and beauty and wisdom of the world; that all men may know that all virtue and all goodness are of him and not of the creature, and that none should glory in his presence, but that he who glories should glory in the Lord to whom is all honour and glory in eternity'. Then Brother Masseo, at this humble and fervent reply, feared within himself and knew certainly that St Francis was grounded in humility. (*L.F.* 10)

Francis took up this question of humility in one of his *Admonitions to the Friars*.

What have you to be proud of? he asked. If you were so clever and learned that you knew everything and could speak every language, so that the things of heaven were an open book to you, still you could not boast of that. Any of the devils knew more about the things of heaven, and knows more about the things of earth, than any human being, even one who might have received from God a special revelation of the highest wisdom. If you were the most handsome and richest man in the world, and could work wonders and drive out devils, all that would be something extrinsic to you; it would not belong to you and you could not boast of it. But there is one thing of which we can all boast; we can boast of our humiliations and in taking up daily the holy cross of our Lord Jesus Christ. (*W*.80–1)

And again:

We can never tell how patient or humble a person is when everything is going well with him. But when those who should cooperate with him do the exact opposite, then we can tell. A man has as much patience and humility as he has then, and no more. (*W*. 83)

Just as Francis was terrified of praise, so he was delighted when people spoke of him with contempt. Although, in the later part of his life Francis was very much revered and popularly known as 'the Saint', in the early days he was often misunderstood and despised. There is an account of how he once preached in the centre of Terni in the presence of the bishop and a large crowd of people. The bishop (not knowing his man) tried to say something appreciative of what Francis had done, though he did not, perhaps, choose his words very wisely.

In this latest hour [he said] God has glorified his Church in this poor and despised, simple and unlettered man. For this reason we are bound always to praise the Lord, knowing that he has not done thus for any other nation.

Francis was delighted. Nothing could give him greater pleasure than to be called, in public 'poor, despised and simple'.

When the saint heard these things [we are told] he accepted it with wonderful kindliness that the bishop had judged him to be contemptible in such express

70

words. And when they were entering the church, he fell at the feet of the bishop, saying: 'In truth, lord bishop, you have done me a great favour, for you alone kept the things that are mine unharmed, whereas others take them away from me. Like a discerning man, you have separated, I say, the precious from the worthless, giving praise to God and ascribing to me my worthlessness'. (*2 Cel.* 141)

Francis was determined that he and his friars should not only *feel* humble, but that they should also *live* humbly. They were to be called Friars Minor because he wanted them to be subordinate and inferior to all, to live among the outcasts of society, to rough it with the poor and the homeless, to be overlooked, neglected and despised, to be regarded as stupid, worthless, incompetent, simple-minded men for whom the world could have no respect. That was why he refused to allow the friars to apply for any kind of privilege or honour, even if it were done in order to increase their efficiency and their usefulness. God knew what he was about. He had told Francis how he and his disciples were to live. All that was needed was that they should be faithful to his call.

There were three ways in which the friars were expected to exercise humility – in working, in begging, and in tending the lepers.

When a number of men had thrown in their lot with St Francis, had parted with everything that they possessed, and had vowed themselves never, in any circumstances, to accept any money, the question soon arose as to how they were to get enough to eat. The obvious thing was to offer their labour wherever it was wanted; but this could be done only on condition that they accepted no wages. Food and lodging of a simple kind were permissible, but no money was ever to change hands. So, in the early days, before people came to love and respect the friars, they lived by working on farms or in houses and gardens or anywhere else where there was work to be done. We read of St Francis working in the scullery of a monastery and of Brother Giles carrying faggots of wood or beating walnut-trees. That domestic and other kinds of labour were the normal life of the friars in the early days is clear from the Rule of 1221 where Francis lays down:

The friars who are engaged in the service of lay people for whom they work should not be in charge of money or of the cellar. They are forbidden to accept positions of authority in the houses of their employers, or to take on any job which would give scandal or make them lose their own souls. They should be the least and subordinate to everyone in the house. The friars who have a trade should work at it, provided that it is no obstacle to their spiritual progress and can be practised without scandal. Everyone should remain at the trade and in the position in which he was called. In payment they may accept anything they need, except money. (*W.* 37)

If they failed to find work then the friars were to resort to begging, which Francis used to call 'the table of the Lord'. This was, indeed, a test of their humility. For a man like Brother Bernard of Quintavalle, who had been a wealthy and highly respected citizen of Assisi, or Brothers Peter and Sylvester who were priests, to be seen going from door to door with a beggar's bowl collecting a few crusts and scraps of food was something which some of the friars must have found very hard to accept. But Francis was insistent that every friar should do this, whatever the cost.

The blessed Francis [says Celano] frequently said that a true Friar Minor should not be long without going out to beg alms. 'And the more noble my son is,' he said, 'the more ready should he be to go, for in this way will merits be heaped up for him.' (*2 Cel.* 75)

On another occasion [we are told], when blessed Francis was at St Mary of the Portiuncula, a friar of true spiritual poverty was coming along the street on his way back from Assisi with alms, and as he walked he was cheerfully singing God's praises in a loud voice. As he drew near the church of St Mary, blessed Francis heard him, and at once went out to meet him with the greatest fervour and joy. He ran up to him in the road and joyfully kissed the shoulder on which he was carrying a bag with alms. Then he took the bag from his shoulder, laid it on his own shoulders, and thus bore it into the friary. And he told the brethren: 'This is how I want a friar of mine to go out and return with alms, happy, joyful, and praising God'. (*S.P.* 25)

To beg was humiliating to the man who had to do it; but Francis pointed out that to give to those who had plenty an opportunity of providing food for the poor servants of Christ was, in fact, doing them a great kindness.

The third test of humility was, undoubtedly, the hardest of all, for this meant actually living among lepers and looking after them. Everyone hated and feared a leper; and even Francis confessed that, in his youth, if he saw a leper in the distance, he would make off as quickly as possible to avoid the disgust and horror which this disease produced. But when he gave his life to God he knew that he must overcome this repugnance and face the prospect of actually living in the filth and stench of a leper-house.

This conquest of himself was something which Francis felt very strongly, as he refers to it in the opening words of his *Testament*.

This is how God inspired me, Brother Francis, to embark upon a life of penance [he wrote]. When I was in sin, the sight of lepers nauseated me beyond measure; but then God himself led me into their company, and I had pity on them. When I had once become acquainted with them, what had previously nauseated me became a source of spiritual and physical consolation for me. After that I did not wait long before leaving the world. (*W.* 67)

To overcome the fear and loathing which he had felt at the sight of a leper, and actually to go into their filthy huts to eat and drink and sleep with them and to tend their sores, this was what Francis meant by humility. And what he had done he demanded also of all those who would follow him.

From the first days of his conversion [we read] blessed Francis, like a wise builder, established himself with God's help on the firm rock of the perfect humility and poverty of the Son of God. And because of his own profound humility, he called his Order that of Friars Minor.

So at the beginning of the Order he wished the friars to live in leper-houses to serve them, and by doing so to establish themselves in holy humility. For whenever anyone, whether noble or commoner, entered the Order, among the other instructions given to him, he was told that he must humbly serve the lepers and live with them as was laid down in the Rule. (*S.P.* 44)

Humility, internal and external, was, then, the first foundation-stone of the Franciscan way of life, and Francis was always grateful to anyone who reminded him of this and warned him not to think of himself more highly than he ought to think. As Celano writes:

Not only did the man of God show himself humble

before his superiors; but also among his equals, and those beneath him, he was more ready to be admonished and corrected than to give admonitions. Wherefore when one day he was riding on an ass, because, weak and infirm as he was, he could not go by foot, he passed through the field of a peasant who happened to be working there just then. The peasant ran over to him and asked solicitously if he were Brother Francis. When the man of God humbly replied that he was the man he was asking about, the peasant said: 'Try to be as good as you are said to be by all men, for many put their trust in you. Therefore I admonish you never to be other than you are expected to be'. When the man of God heard this, he got down from the ass and threw himself before the peasant and humbly kissed his feet, thanking him for being kind enough to give him this warning. (*2 Cel.* 142)

Simplicity

Thomas of Celano describes Francis's love of simplicity in these words:

The saint was zealous with more than usual care to show forth in himself, and he loved in others, holy simplicity, the daughter of grace, the sister of wisdom, the mother of justice. Not all simplicity, however, was approved by him, but only that simplicity which, being content with its God, considers everything else as of little value. This is that simplicity that glories in the fear of God, that knows not how to do or to speak evil. This is that simplicity that, examining itself, condemns no one by its judgement; and that, surrendering due authority to a better, seeks no authority for itself. This is that simplicity that, in all the divine laws,

75

leaves wordy circumlocutions, ornaments and embellishments, vain displays and curiosities, to those who are marked for a fall, and seeks not the bark but the pith, not the shell but the kernel, not the many things, but the much, the greatest and the lasting good. (*2 Cel.* 189)

This simplicity expressed itself in many ways. In the first place it meant a very simple approach to the words of Christ. Francis would never wish to argue over any reported saying of Christ; still less to try to adapt it to suit his own convenience or that of his brethren. For example, on hearing that Jesus had forbidden his disciples to possess two coats, Francis expected all his friars to do the same, though, in course of time, some concessions had to be made if these men were to survive the colder climates of places like Scotland and Scandinavia. But Francis never really approved of this. In his *Testament* he declares that, in the early days, he and his companions had always been satisfied with but one habit, even if, sometimes, it had been totally inadequate to resist the cold winds of the Apennines. A little-known story tells how St Francis

when walking along a road in a biting wind, felt himself becoming fainthearted. So he summoned up courage and, climbing a hill, took off his clothes and turned to face the wind. Then he told himself that it would be well for him if he had even one habit. (*N.F.* 30)

So it was with everything that Christ had said. Francis would willingly have cut off his hand or his foot if he thought they were leading him to destruction; and he took Christ's command to 'take no thought for the morrow' with the utmost seriousness.

While blessed Francis was with the first friars [says the *Mirror of Perfection*] he lived with them in such poverty that they observed the holy Gospel to the letter in all things and through all things, from the very day when our Lord revealed to him that he and his friars were to live according to the pattern of the holy Gospel. He therefore forbade the friar who cooked for the brethren to put dried beans into warm water in the evening, as is usual, when he intended to give them to the friars to eat on the following day. This was in order to observe the saying of the holy Gospel: 'Take no thought for the morrow'. So the friar delayed putting them to soften until after Mattins on the day when they were to be eaten. Many friars, especially in towns, continued to observe this custom for a long time, and would not seek or accept more alms than were necessary to support them for a single day. (*S.P.* 19)

Another mark of the simplicity of St Francis was his innocence. There was, in his eyes, no distinction to be drawn between the deserving and the undeserving poor. Anyone who came and asked for his help was rewarded so long as he had anything to give. He was remarkably shrewd in his attitude to the friars, often reading their thoughts with uncanny accuracy, and spotting any sign of insincerity or hypocrisy on their part; but towards people in general he was always extremely generous, believing the hard-luck stories of the beggars and seeing Christ in every man who was in need of help.

Again, he had a very simple faith in the providence of God. When something like five thousand friars assembled at the Portiuncula, some people became very anxious as to how they were to be fed. But Francis had no worry on that score. God will provide; and, of course, he did by sending crowds of men and women down the hill from

Assisi loaded with bread, and fruit and fish for the use of the friars. On one such occasion so much food was provided that the friars had to stay on for an extra two days to eat it all up.

This kind of simple faith shows itself very clearly in his behaviour in the East. He had travelled to Egypt in order to try to put an end to the Crusades by converting the Soldan to the Christian faith. To do this he would have to talk to the Soldan personally; and this would mean leaving the Christian lines and crossing the open country in order to penetrate into the camp of the Saracen army. When Francis announced that this was his intention he was laughed to scorn. Everyone knew that any Christian who fell into the hands of the Moslems would be instantly killed. But Francis had no fear. The Lord would look after him if he approved of his mission, as he must surely do. Francis did not succeed in converting the Soldan to the Christian faith; but he said what he wanted to say to him and was given a safe-conduct to ensure his return to the Christian lines unharmed.

And so it was all the time. Francis had put himself into the hands of God, and God would take care of him if he had work for him to do. The one essential thing was that Francis's trust should never falter. All the rest he could leave safely to God.

There was no battle which Francis found it harder to fight under the banner of Simplicity than the struggle against those of his friars who wanted more opportunity for study in order that the friars might, as they thought, become more qualified as preachers and so of greater service to the Church and to mankind. Francis was not opposed to scholarship, but he was quite sure that this was not an essential ingredient of the way of life to which he and his disciples were called. Other Orders, like the Order of Preachers, could deal with that. But not all his friars agreed with him. In the early days the brotherhood was composed almost entirely of laymen; but, as the years went by, more and more priests and scholars joined it. Many men who had been educated, even up to the standard then required for the priesthood, would want to continue their studies to some extent; while some of those who became Friars Minor were among the most learned scholars in the world, men like Bonaventura, Roger Bacon, Duns Scotus, and many more. These were men who had much to give in the realm of teaching and of preaching; but they could not give of their best unless they had access to books and places in which to read and write. So, for most of Francis's life, there was considerable tension between those pleading for the modest requirements of the trained teacher and those who were determined that this should not be allowed for the sake of simplicity.

The way of life which Francis had chosen really made any kind of serious scholarship virtually impossible, since it was bound to transgress the restrictions of total poverty. But Francis saw it also as a breach of simplicity. His friars were called to be 'unlearned and subject to all'. He did not want them to be praised for the brilliance of their sermons or for the wisdom of their writings.

Blessed Francis [we are told] was very grieved whenever he found virtue neglected in favour of the sort of learning that brings pride, especially if anyone was not persevering in the vocation to which he had first been called. He used to say: 'Friars of mine who are seduced by a desire for learning will find their hands empty in the day of trouble. I would rather have them grow stronger in virtue, so that when the time of trial comes, they will have God with them in their struggle. For a troublous time is coming when books will be no good for anything and will be cast aside in windows and corners'. He did not say this because the study of Holy Scripture displeased him, but to restrain all the friars from a useless preoccupation with learning. He would rather have them excel in charity than in strange forms of knowledge. (*S.P.* 69)

and in his 'Praises of all the Virtues' he wrote:

Pure and holy Simplicity puts all the learning of this world, all natural wisdom, to shame. (*W.* 133)

Francis thought that the learning which a man had acquired was one of the things which he ought to be prepared to surrender if he accepted the call to be a Friar Minor. As he once said:

A great cleric must in some way give up even his learning when he comes to the Order, so that, having renounced such a possession he may offer himself naked to the arms of the Crucified. (*2 Cel.* 194)

In Francis's eyes poverty, humility and simplicity were all at risk if a man wanted to devote his time to scholarship even on a modest scale. He was convinced that the only way to teach people about God was to live an exemplary life based on the teaching of Jesus; and all that this required was access to the Gospels. So, all through his life, Francis struggled to maintain what was, to him, a fundamental issue. His opponents were strong, led by Cardinal Ugolino, the Protector of the Order, who persuaded some of the friars to plead with Francis for some relaxation. Ugolino was anxious to use the immensely influential force which Francis had created for the greatest benefit of the Church. To have a number of good scholars and teachers who were prepared to live a simple life and to go anywhere to fulfil their ministry was an opportunity not to be lightly thrown away. But Francis knew his own mind and would not give in.

Angelo Clareno, a later disciple of St Francis, wrote:

Some French friars once came to St Francis and told him that, at Paris, the brethren had appointed as their master a learned professor of theology who had greatly edified both clergy and laity. But when St Francis heard this he sighed and said: 'I am afraid, brothers, that such men will end by killing my little plant. The true masters are those who set a good example to their neighbours in good works and kindness; for a man is learned just inasmuch as he loves God and his neighbour; and he is a good preacher just inasmuch as he knows how to do good works, faithfully and humbly'. (*N.F.* 14)

These words, recorded more than a century after St Francis had lived, show why he had this dread of learning, the chief enemy of his beloved Simplicity.

Poverty

To most people poverty is essentially a negative thing. To be poor means to be without the things which most people seek after – money, the necessities of life, security, respectability, and so on. To accept poverty cheerfully might be regarded as virtuous; to desire poverty might be thought abnormal and eccentric; while to make poverty an ideal to be fought for with all your strength would be considered unintelligible.

Francis was brought up in a wealthy home; but gradually step by step, he was led to give up everything and adopt a life of such extreme poverty that he literally owned nothing. He was not, of course, alone in this. There have always been people who are virtually without anything that they can call their own – slaves, tramps, paupers – but all of these have been regarded as unfortunate, the dregs of society, whether their poverty is brought about by their failures or by the evil done to them by other men.

Francis discovered poverty by means of a series of experiences spread over some years. His future became clear when he heard the words of Christ read to him in the little church of the Portiuncula on the feast of St Matthias, and it arose out of his conception of obedience. By this time he had already made up his mind to obey every command of Christ, however difficult this might be, and however great the cost. Jesus had warned people over and over again of the danger of riches, and he had called on those who wished to follow him to get rid of their possessions. 'Whosoever of you does not renounce all that he has cannot be my disciple', he had said. Francis saw this as a statement which cannot be explained or ignored. And so, gradually, he proceeded to get rid of everything that he possessed, ending up by giving back to his father not only his money but also his clothes, so that, for a moment, he stood naked and totally destitute until the kindly Bishop of Assisi wrapped him in his own cloak.

Francis was determined, from then onwards, to show the world that absolute poverty was something that man could enjoy. It was not, in his mind, something negative, still less something to be avoided. To him poverty became an ideal, a state of bliss to be worked for and paid for. Just as it took hard work, effort and concentration in order to get rich, so it required the same qualities in order to get poor and to stay poor. Francis had seen the trouble to which his father had gone to make money, and he was prepared now to take just as much trouble to become poor. 'Poverty', said St Bonaventura, 'was his profession', something to work for, something which demanded skill and intense application.

Once Francis had accepted poverty as an ideal, he began to clothe it with the language of imagination and romance. To be destitute was to cast oneself upon God, to depend upon him as a small child depends upon its parents for everything. While other men were tied down by the burden of making a living, Francis was free to enjoy what God gave him. As the Franciscan poet, Jacopone of Todi, wrote in later years:

> Poverty is to have nothing,
> And to desire nothing;
> And yet to possess everything,
> In the spirit of liberty.

or, as Bonaventura wrote:

Among the supernatural gifts which Francis received from God, the generous Giver, his love for absolute poverty constituted a special privilege which enabled him to grow rich in spiritual wealth. He saw that it had been the constant companion of the Son of God, but that now it was scorned by the whole world, and so he espoused it in undying love. For poverty's sake he abandoned his father and his mother and divested himself of everything that he had. No one was so greedy for gold as he was for poverty; no treasure was guarded so jealously as he guarded this Gospel pearl. (*Bon.* vii, 1)

To Francis, then, poverty was not only an ideal but a source of joy. Poverty brought one into union with God in a special way. It had been the companion of Christ in his earthly life, and commended by him as the way of discipleship. Poverty was, therefore, the highest form of life which anyone could hope to achieve. All this comes out in the thirteenth chapter of the *Little Flowers* which records how Francis and Brother Masseo, when they were on a missionary journey, stopped at a town to beg for some food as they were very hungry. When they had collected a little food, Francis cried out: 'O Brother

Masseo, we are not worthy of so great treasure'; to which
Masseo replied:

> 'Father, how can this be called treasure, when we are
> in such poverty, and lack the things of which we have
> need; we, who have neither cloth, nor knives, nor
> plates, nor bowl, nor house, nor table, nor manservant
> nor maidservant?' Then said St Francis: 'This is what
> I call a great treasure, that there is nothing here
> provided by human industry, but everything is provid-
> ed by Divine Providence, as we may see manifestly in
> this bread which we have begged, in this stone which
> serves so beautifully for our table, and in this so clear
> fountain; and therefore I desire that we should pray to
> God that he would cause holy poverty, which is a
> thing so noble that God himself was made subject to
> it, to be loved by us with our whole heart'. And when
> he had said these words, and they had made their
> prayer, and partaken for bodily refreshment of the
> pieces of bread, and drunk of the water, they arose and
> went on their way. (*L.F.* 13)

Shortly afterwards Francis added these words:

> My brother, let us go to St Peter and St Paul and pray
> them to teach us and to give us to possess the im-
> measurable treasure of holy poverty, inasmuch as it is
> a treasure so exalted and so divine that we are not
> worthy to possess it in our vile bodies, seeing that this
> is that celestial virtue by which all earthly and tran-
> sitory things are trodden under foot and all im-
> pediments are lifted away from the soul, so that she
> can freely unite herself to the eternal God. And this is
> the virtue which makes the soul, while still retained on
> earth, converse with the angels in heaven, and this it is
> which accompanied Christ to his cross, with Christ
> was buried, with Christ was raised up, with Christ

ascended into heaven; which, being given in this life to the souls who are enamoured of it, facilitates their flight to heaven, seeing that it guards the arms of true humility and charity. And therefore let us pray the most holy apostles of Christ, who were perfect lovers of this pearl of the Gospel of Christ, that they will beg for us this grace from our Lord Jesus Christ, that by his most holy mercy he would grant us the merit to be true lovers, observers and humble disciples of this most precious, most lovable, evangelical poverty. (ibid.)

Poverty, then, was, to St Francis, a treasure to be sought, the 'pearl of great price', something so valuable and desirable that a man will sell all that he has in order to obtain it. This jewel Francis went on to clothe with human flesh. Poverty became to him the 'Lady Poverty', the object of his love and devotion. As the romantic poets and the troubadours sang the praises of their beloved – the most beautiful and most desirable of all women – so Francis spoke of his Lady Poverty, not only as the lady most worthy of our love, but also as the person most deeply loved by Christ.

Celano writes:

At times the saint would repeat: 'In as far as the brothers depart from poverty, insomuch will the world depart from them; and they will seek', he said, 'and will not find. But if they embrace my Lady Poverty, the world will provide for them, because they have been given to the world unto its salvation'. (*2 Cel.* 70)

Francis liked to feel that there was a kind of contract or bond between the friars and Lady Poverty. She was their patron, the one whom they must love and serve faithfully and diligently. So long as they did this all would go well; but if they deserted her, or broke their contract, then evil would fall upon them. Francis fought for poverty all through his life. It was a hard battle, for the demands of Lady Poverty were great and not easily to be met. But Francis won through; and when he lay dying on the rough floor of a little hut near the church of the Portiuncula he made the friars take away all his clothes so that he could lie 'naked upon the naked earth'. It was then that his spirits rose to their highest pitch and he 'was glad out of the gladness of his heart, for he saw that he had kept faith with Lady Poverty to the end'. (*2 Cel.* 215)

This romantic courtship between Francis and Lady Poverty was the theme of what is believed to be the first tract written about him after his death. It was called *The Holy Converse of Francis with Lady Poverty* and is a romantic story of how Francis sought out the poor, despised and hated Lady Poverty and made her his bride. He loved her dearly, not only for her own virtue and beauty, but because she had been Christ's most faithful friend, the only one who stood by him to the end. Francis addresses her in these terms:

> You alone clung to the King of Glory when all his chosen and loved ones timidly abandoned him. You, however, a most faithful spouse, a most tender lover, did not for a moment leave him; what is more, you clung to him all the more faithfully the more you saw him despised by all others. You were with him when all the Jews reviled him, when the Pharisees insulted him, when the chief priests cursed him; you were with him when he was buffeted, spat upon and scourged. He who should have been respected by all was mocked by all, and you alone comforted him. You did not leave him unto death, even to death on a cross. And on the cross itself, when he hung there naked, his arms outstretched, his hands and feet pierced, you suffered with him, so that nothing in him should appear more glorious than you. (*Holy Converse,* 20–1)

This, of course, was written after Francis's death; but, had he seen it, he would have accepted it as a faithful interpretation of his love for poverty, the Bride of Christ.

Like all high ideals, poverty was something which demanded great self-sacrifice and endless care. Francis knew how easy it would be to lose track of his beloved, to drift away from her embraces, to fail in his devotion. In the early days, when the brotherhood consisted only of a handful of men, inspired by the example of Francis and willing to suffer anything in the pursuit of their ideal, it was fairly easy to keep faith with Lady Poverty. They were often hungry and cold. They had only very scanty clothing and nowhere to find shelter except in caves, huts and empty churches. They never knew where their next meal would come from, or even whether there would be a next meal. They might easily have died of starvation in those early days when no one understood what they were trying to do. But they were determined to go forward, even if it led them to a painful death.

At one point the Bishop of Assisi thought it right to warn them of the dangers which they were facing.

> 'It seems to me', he said, 'that it is very hard and difficult to possess nothing in the world.' To this blessed Francis replied: 'My lord, if we had any possessions we should also be forced to have arms to protect them, since possessions are a cause of disputes and strife, and in many ways we should be hindered from loving God and our neighbours. Therefore in this life we wish to have no temporal possessions'. The Bishop was greatly pleased by these words of God's servant; and indeed Francis despised all passing things, especially money, so much so that he laid the greatest stress on holy poverty and insisted that the brothers should be most careful to avoid money. (*3 Soc.* 35)

Francis realised that if any of the friars accepted

money then the contract with Lady Poverty would be broken and her trust in them betrayed. As Celano says:

> That friend of God despised very greatly all the things of this world, but he cursed money more than all other things. Consequently, from the beginning of his conversion, he held it in special contempt and always said that it was to be shunned as the devil himself. (*2 Cel.* 65)

This hatred of money became something of an obsession in Francis's mind, and any friar who, for whatever reason, touched a coin was liable to be severely punished either by Francis or by God himself. A friar, finding some money left by some well-wisher on the altar of the church of the Portiuncula, picked it up and threw it on to the window-sill. Francis, hearing of this, ordered him to take the money in his mouth and put it on a heap of dung outside. Another friar who picked up a coin lying in the road in order to give it to some lepers, lost his speech. (*2 Cel.* 65–6) Francis expressed his wishes very clearly in the Rule of 1221:

> All the friars, no matter where they are or where they go, are forbidden to take or accept money in any way or under any form, or have it accepted for them, for clothing or books, or as wages, or in any other necessity, except to provide for the urgent needs of those who are ill. We should have no more use or regard for money in any of its forms than for dust. Those who think it is worth more or who are greedy for it, expose themselves to the danger of being deceived by the devil. We have left everything we had behind us; we must be very careful now not to lose the kingdom of heaven for so little. (*W.*38)

Needless to say, this had to be somewhat relaxed in

later legislation when the Order had grown so large and problems had arisen which Francis had not conceived of in the early days.

To Francis, poverty was an ideal to be worked for, guarded, and cherished. There were several reasons for this. In the first place, it was the way of life chosen by Christ, and therefore the highest and noblest of all professions; as St Francis described it, 'naked to follow the naked Christ'. Secondly, it was a form of self-sacrifice, a denial of the normal human instincts in order that life may be offered to God. Thirdly, it made man dependent upon God rather than upon his own resources, so deepening his trust. Lastly, it gave other people the opportunity of showing charity to those who had adopted this way of life.

Francis's battle against those who would not accept this ideal was long and painful. As the Order grew and became more stabilised, some security became necessary. The friars soon found that they had to have somewhere to live. Francis wanted them to live, summer and winter, in little huts which they made out of the branches of trees; but this became impossible when the Order spread into northern Europe, and when it became more clericalised and academic. But Francis put up considerable resistance to those who would not do as he wished. Arriving one day at Bologna, and finding that a house had been specially built for the friars, he refused to go into it and ordered all the friars living there to leave immediately including the sick. At the Portiuncula, which St Francis carried in his heart as the most sacred place of all, he found that the people of Assisi, out of their goodwill towards the friars, had built them a house made of stone and mortar. When he discovered this, he climbed on the roof and started to dismantle the place until he was stopped by some armed men who told him that the building belonged to the Commune of Assisi and not to the friars. (*S.P.* 6–7) At one of the centres to which the friars resorted, one of them made the mistake of putting up for Francis a little wooden hut where he could go to say his prayers. When Francis arrived, he took one look at it and refused to go near it. 'This cell is too fine', he said. 'If you wish me to stay here, have a cell made with branches and ferns as its only covering inside and out.' So this was done, and Francis was persuaded to stay for a bit. But when another of the friars, in talking to Francis, innocently referred to 'your cell', Francis was extremely indignant and exclaimed: 'Because you have called it mine, someone else shall use it in future and not I'. (*S.P.* 9)

So it was with food and clothing, furniture and bedding. Francis insisted that the friars should have only the barest food, begged often from the houses of the poor and therefore little more than they would have thrown out to the birds. He was adamant that the clothes which the friars wore should be ragged, patched and shabby as he felt it a disgrace to appear better off than the poorest person he might chance to meet on the road. Beds were not allowed, and the friars slept on a little straw spread on the floor.

Such was the ideal; but it was not always observed as rigidly as Francis would have wished. One of the friars tells the following story:

When one of the Friar-Ministers had visited blessed Francis in order to keep the feast of Christmas with him in the friary in Rieti, the friars prepared the tables rather elaborately and carefully on Christmas Day in honour of the Minister, putting on fair white linen and glass vessels. But when the Father came down from his cell to eat, and saw the tables raised up from the ground and prepared with such great care, he went back secretly and took the hat and staff of a poor beggar who had arrived that day. And calling in a low voice to one of his companions, he went out of the door of the friary unseen by the brethren in the house, while his companion remained inside near the door. Meanwhile the friars came in to dine, for blessed Francis had ordered that, whenever he did not come at once at mealtime, the friars were not to wait for him.

When he had stood outside for a while, he knocked on the door and his companion immediately opened to him. And entering with his hat on his back and his staff in his hand, he came like a stranger or beggar to the door of the room where the friars were eating, and called out: 'For the love of God, give alms to this poor, sick stranger'. But the Minister and the other friars recognised him at once. And the Minister replied: 'Brother, we are poor as well, and because we are so many, the alms that we have only meet our needs. But for the love of God which you have invoked, come in and we will share with you the alms which the Lord has given us'.

When he had entered and stood before the friars' table, the Minister handed to him the plate from which he was eating, and also some bread. And taking it, Francis humbly sat down on the floor beside the fire in the sight of the friars sitting at the table. Then he sighed and said to the brethren: 'When I saw the table elaborately and carefully laid, I felt that this was not the table of poor religious who go around for alms from door to door each day. Dearest brothers, we are under a greater obligation than other religious to follow the example of Christ's humility and poverty, for it is to this end that we have been called and professed before God and men. So it seems to me that it is I who am sitting like a Friar Minor, because the feasts of our Lord and the Saints are better honoured in the want and poverty by which these Saints won heaven, than in the luxury and excess by which a soul is estranged from heaven'. (*S.P.* 20)

On another occasion Francis found himself invited to sit down to a meal in Rome with the Bishop of Ostia. Here was a new kind of problem and perhaps a new opportunity for Francis to show his devotion to Lady Poverty. When the time for dinner drew near

he went out for alms, and returning placed some of the scraps of black bread on the bishop's table. When the bishop saw this he was somewhat ashamed, above all because of the newly invited guests. The father, however, with a joyous countenance distributed the alms which he had received to the knights and chaplains gathered about the table. All of them accepted the alms with wonderful devotion, and some of them ate them, others kept them out of reverence. When the dinner was finished, the bishop arose; and, taking the man of God to an inner room, he raised his arms and embraced him. 'My brother,' he said, 'why did you bring shame on me in the house that is yours and your brothers, by going out for alms?' The saint said to him: 'Rather I have shown you honour, for I have honoured a greater lord. For the Lord is well pleased with poverty, and above all with that poverty that is voluntary. For I have a royal dignity and a special nobility, namely, to follow the Lord who, being rich, became poor for us'. And he added: 'I get more delight from a poor table that is furnished with small alms than from great tables on which dainty foods are placed almost without number'. Then, greatly edified, the bishop said to the saint: 'Son, do what seems good in your eyes, for the Lord is with you'. (*2 Cel.* 73);

and the Lord was indeed with him, giving him courage and grace to fulfil his ambition and to keep faith with Lady Poverty to the end.

Prayer

Humility and Simplicity were states of mind, and Poverty was a way of life. All three demanded great industry and application, so great that Francis knew well enough that there was no hope of achieving them without the help of God. It was inevitable, therefore, that the fourth foundation-stone of his life should be Prayer – the constant and, indeed, virtually continuous contact with God – upon which everything else depended. Bonaventura writes:

Saint Francis realised that he was an exile from the Lord's presence as long as he was at home in the body, and his love of Christ had left him with no desire for the things of this earth. Therefore he tried to keep his spirit always in the presence of God, by praying to him without intermission, so that he might not be without some comfort from his Beloved. Prayer was his chief comfort in this life of contemplation in which he became a fellow-citizen of the angels, as he penetrated the dwelling places of heaven in his eager search for his Beloved, from whom he was separated only by a partition of flesh. Prayer was his sure refuge in everything that he did; he never relied on his own efforts, but put his trust in God's loving providence and cast the burden of his cares on him in insistent prayer. He was convinced that the grace of prayer was something that a religious should long for above all else. No one, he declared, could make progress in God's service without it; and he used every means he could to make the friars concentrate on it. Whether he was walking or sitting, at home or abroad, whether he was working or resting, he was so fervently devoted to prayer that he seemed to have dedicated to it not only his heart and his soul, but all his efforts and all his time. (*Bon.* x, 1)

and Celano says:

His safest haven was prayer; not prayer of a single moment, or idle or presumptuous prayer, but prayer of long duration, full of devotion, serene in humility. If he began late, he would scarcely finish before morning. Walking, sitting, eating or drinking, he was always intent upon prayer. He would go alone to pray at night in churches abandoned and located in deserted places, where, under the protection of divine grace, he overcame many fears and many disturbances of mind. (*1 Cel.* 71)

As a member of a religious Order, Francis felt himself committed to saying the daily Offices of the Church. In the early days this was not always easy. Absolute poverty made it impossible for the friars to possess Office-books; and they had, therefore, to depend upon finding the books they needed in parish churches or elsewhere. Some of the friars found this very inconvenient. Priest-friars naturally wanted to keep their vows; and breviaries were not always to be found in the country churches which they passed on their travels. But Francis was adamant on this point, three times reproving a young friar who asked for permission to have a copy of the Psalter which he could call his own. (*S.P.* 4) Yet, somehow or other, Francis managed to say his Offices with regularity and devotion.

Although he had been troubled for many years by his infirmities [writes the *Mirror of Perfection*] Francis was so devout and reverent at prayer and the Divine Office that whenever he was at prayer or reciting the Divine Office he would never lean against a wall or support.

He always stood upright and bareheaded, although he sometimes knelt. Indeed, he devoted the greater part of the day and night to prayer, and even when he was travelling around on foot, he would always halt when he wished to say the Hours. But if he were riding because of his infirmity, he would always dismount to say the Office.

One day it was raining heavily, and he was riding because of his infirmity and pressing need. And although he was already drenched to the skin, he dismounted from the horse when he wished to say the Hours, and said the Office standing in the road with the rain pouring down on him, as though he had been in a church or cell. And he said to his companion: 'If the body likes to take its food in peace and at ease, although it becomes food for worms, how much greater should be the soul's reverence and devotion when it receives the food which is God himself'. (*S.P.* 94)

In later years some relaxation on the question of Office-books seems to have been made; for, in the Rule of 1221, Francis lays it down that the friars 'may have those books which are necessary for their religious exercises'. (*W.34*) He himself actually acquired a breviary in later life, given to him by two of the brothers.

When he was well [writes Brother Leo] he liked to say the Office regularly, as is written in the Rule. And when he was ill and could not say it, he liked to hear it said. This he kept up as long as he lived. Moreover, he had the Gospels written out; and when, either through sickness or for any other obvious reason, he could not hear Mass, he had read to him the Gospel for the day as it was read in church. . . And when the blessed Francis had either read or heard the Gospel he always used to kiss the book with the utmost reverence. (*N.F.* 49)

Inevitably the prayer-life of the friars had to be different from that of other religious. Members of the monastic Orders were provided not only with churches in which they could pray, but also with the necessary books for their Offices; while Bibles, commentaries and books of devotion were normally to be found in their libraries. But the friar had none of these facilities, since he was an itinerant preacher who carried nothing with him. Most of his praying must therefore be spontaneous and personal. When Francis sent out his disciples he said to them:

> Take the road two and two in the name of the Lord. Be humble and sincere. Keep silence from dawn until after Terce, praying to God in your hearts, and do not indulge in idle and unprofitable conversation. Although you are travelling, let your words be as humble and devout as in a hermitage or a cell. For wherever we are, or wherever we go, we always take our cell with us; for Brother Body is our cell, and our soul is the hermit who lives in it, constantly praying to God and meditating on him. If the soul cannot remain quiet in its cell, then a cell made with hands is of little value to a Religious. (*S.P.* 65)

Francis himself liked to find quiet places in which to pray; but, when this was not possible, he was able to detach himself completely from what was going on around him and pray with total absorption. As Celano says:

> He always sought a hidden place where he could adapt not only his soul but also all his members to God. When he suddenly felt himself visited by the Lord in public, lest he be without a cell he made a cell of his cloak. At times when he did not have a cloak he would cover his face with his sleeve so that he would

not disclose the hidden manna. Always he put something between himself and the bystanders lest they should become aware of the Bridegroom's touch. Thus he could pray unseen even among many people in the narrow confines of a ship. Finally, when he could not do any of these things, he would make a temple of his breast. (*2 Cel*. 94)

Francis never made any decision, however trivial, without prolonged prayer. Often he would spend a whole night in prayer. From time to time he would retire to some quiet place – a cave in a wood, or an island, where he knew that he would not be disturbed – and there prayed for long hours on end. These 'retreats' generally lasted for five or six weeks, occupying the whole of Lent or the period from the Feast of the Assumption until Michaelmas. Much of the time would be spent in what Bonaventura called 'the restful ecstasy of contemplation' (*Bon*. xiii, 1), but Francis would also devote himself to intercession for the brothers, or people whom he knew to be in need, or for the Church. Sometimes he expressed his petitions in the form of words, sometimes silently. At times he cried aloud: 'filling the woods with sighs, watering the ground with his tears and striking his breast with his hand'. (*2 Cel*. 94) Often he would just repeat a short phrase over and over again throughout the night, rapt in contemplation of the glory and majesty of God and of his own shortcomings. When Bernard of Quintavalle invited Francis to spend a night with him in his house in Assisi, he lay awake all night while Francis knelt on the floor saying nothing but 'My God and my all'. (*L.F*. 2) On another occasion he prayed for a very long time saying only 'God be merciful to me a sinner'. (*1 Cel*. 26) Again, he once spent a whole night saying nothing but 'O most holy Lord, I long to love thee. O most sweet Lord, I long to love thee'. (*N.F*. 51)

Often his prayers took the form of a violent struggle

with the powers of evil, for Francis felt himself to be surrounded at all times by devils trying to drag his soul into
hell. During many of his long vigils he would be so much
battered and bruised that he could scarcely stand.

Not only [says Celano] was this man attacked by
Satan with temptations, but he even carried on a
hand-to-hand battle with him. Once when he had
been asked by the Lord Cardinal Leo of the Holy
Cross to stay with him for a little while in Rome, he
chose a certain secluded tower that was divided by
nine arched vaults into what looked like small cells for
hermits. The first night, therefore, when he wanted to
rest, after he had poured out his prayers to God, the
devils came and made preparations for a hostile
struggle with the saint of God. They beat him for a
long time very severely and in the end left him as
though half dead. After they had gone and he had
recovered his breath, the saint called his companion
who was sleeping under one of the other arched vaults
and said to him when he came: 'Brother, I would like
you to stay near me because I am afraid to be alone.
For the devils beat me a little time ago'. The saint was
trembling and shaking in his members, like a person
suffering a severe fever. (*2 Cel.* 119)

Apart from the short prayers which Francis is known
to have spoken in his long periods of vigil, we know very
little of what words came to him in his prayers. Among
his writings there is a prayer which says:

May the power of your love, O Lord, fiery and sweet
as honey, wean my heart from all that is under heaven,
so that I may die for love of your love, you who were so
good as to die for love of my love. (*W.* 161)

But there is very little evidence that this is an authentic

work of the saint. The prayer which begins with the words: 'Lord, make me an instrument of thy peace' and which is often called 'The Prayer of St Francis' is, in fact, a modern compilation which has no immediate connection with St Francis, though, in many ways, it expresses ideas very much in keeping with his teaching.

It is, perhaps, not surprising that we know so little about the way in which St Francis prayed. Apart from the daily Offices, his devotions did not normally take the form of set prayers. This was not his style. We know that sometimes he repeated short sentences over and over again; but, for much of his praying, words were not necessary. In his prayers, petition, adoration and contemplation were all fused together. Thomas of Celano describes his prayers in these words:

All his attention and affection he directed with his whole being to the one thing which he was asking of the Lord, not so much praying as becoming himself a prayer. (*2 Cel.* 95)

5. OBEDIENCE AND JOY

Life, for St Francis, was extremely complicated. He set out to live, alone, a life based entirely on the teaching of Christ as recorded in the Gospels. This made great demands on his courage and his faith, but he was fully prepared to pay the price. It was, however, not long before he found that there were others, both men and women, who declared themselves ready to join him in his great adventure. This created new problems. Would they be able to face the dangers and bear the pains and humiliations which he bore? Francis tested each one individually, and accepted them only if he was satisfied of their integrity and determination. The real trouble, however, arose when large numbers of men flocked to join his little company of itinerant preachers, each one of whom was vowed to total poverty and humility, with the result that a large religious Order, with settlements all over Europe, sprang into existence, creating immense problems of organisation and discipline. Was it now conceivable that the abnormally high standards would continue; or was there bound to be some relaxation? Could an army of some five thousand men (and a considerable number of women) continue to live without property or security of any kind? Francis was determined to preserve his ideals of Poverty, Humility and Simplicity if it was humanly possible. But he was fully aware of the difficulties and dangers as his little brotherhood grew almost out of all recognition.

Francis saw that the key to hold them all together and save the Order from drifting into mediocrity, or even worse, was the virtue of Obedience – obedience to God, obedience to the ideals which Francis had adopted, and obedience to authority in the Order whether spoken or written. In his 'Praises of the Virtues' he wrote:

> Holy Obedience puts to shame
> all natural and selfish desires.
> It mortifies our lower nature
> and makes it obey the spirit and our fellow men. (*W.* 133)

Only when a man had surrendered his life to God, and, at the same time, had gained complete mastery over himself could he understand the virtue of Obedience.

In the Rule of 1221 Francis wrote:

> No matter where they are, the friars must always remember that they have given themselves up completely and handed over their whole selves to our Lord Jesus Christ; and so they should be prepared to expose themselves to every enemy, visible or invisible, for love of him. (*W.* 44)

And in one of his letters he pointed out that the obedience which man owes to God is none other than the obedience which Christ gave to the Father.

> Our Lord Jesus Christ [he wrote] gave his life rather than fail in the obedience he owed to his most holy Father. (*W.* 108)

The first obedience, then, was obedience to God. Whatever Francis thought to be the will of God, that he wished to obey at all costs. Life, apart from this, meant nothing to him. He regarded the flesh and all its natural

desires as the enemy of the soul, something against which
to strive continuously, watching with the greatest
vigilance for every approach of the forces which were trying to make him give ground.

Everyone [he wrote] has his own enemy in his power,
and this enemy is his lower nature which leads him
into sin. Blessed the religious who keeps this enemy a
prisoner under his control and protects himself against
it. As long as he does this, no other enemy, visible or
invisible, can harm him. (*W*. 82)

To some of us, living only in the spiritual lowlands,
Francis's war against his own body may seem ex-
aggerated and even unnatural and unwise. But to him it
was essential, partly out of love for Christ who had suffered so much on our behalf, and partly to set a good example to those who looked to him as their leader. As St
Bonaventura writes:

When Francis saw that great numbers of lay people
were being inspired by his example to embrace
Christ's cross fervently, he took heart; and, like a
brave leader in Christ's army he determined to carry
off the prize of victory by practising virtue to a heroic
degree. Recalling the words of St Paul, 'those who
belong to Christ have crucified nature with all its
passions, with its impulses', he mortified his lower
appetites so strictly that he scarcely took enough food
or drink to stay alive. In this way he would clothe
himself with the armour of the Cross. He used to say
that it was hard to satisfy one's material needs without
giving in to the inclinations of sensuality. As long as he
enjoyed good health he scarcely ever ate cooked food.
When he did, he mixed it with ashes or destroyed its
taste, usually by adding water. He never drank
enough water even when he was burning with thirst –

not to mention taking wine – and he devised ways of practising even greater self-denial, becoming better at it day by day. He was already perfect in every way, but still he was always beginning afresh, just as if he were only starting, and he castigated his natural desires by punishing his body . . . More often than not his weary body had only the bare earth for a bed, and he usually slept in an upright position with a piece of wood or a stone at his head. He was content with one worn habit as he served God in cold and nakedness. (*Bon.* v, 1)

A friar once asked him how obedient he had found his body when he expected so much from it. Francis replied:

I bear witness concerning it, son, that it was obedient in all things; it spared itself in nothing, but rushed almost headlong to obey all my commands. It shirked no labour, it refused no discomfort, so long as it could do what was commanded. In this I and it agreed perfectly that we would serve the Lord Christ without any reluctance. (*2 Cel.* 211)

Yet there were moments when he had to admit that he had been a hard taskmaster of what he liked to call 'Brother Ass', and that he had sometimes laid too heavy a load on its back.

Our most holy Father [says the *Mirror of Perfection*], knowing that the body was created to serve the soul, and that bodily actions were to be performed for spiritual ends, used to say: 'In eating, sleeping, and satisfying the other needs of the body, the servant of God should make sensible provision for his Brother Body so that it may not have cause to complain and say "I cannot stand upright and continue at prayer, nor can I be cheerful in my troubles or do other good

103

things, because you do not provide for my needs". But if the servant of God satisfies his body wisely, adequately, and suitably, and Brother Body wants to be careless, fat, and sleepy in prayer, vigils, and other good works, then he must punish him like a fat and idle beast, because he wants to eat but not to be useful and carry his load'. (*S.P.* 97)

While it was possible for an individual with Francis's determination and courage to keep up a high standard of self-discipline in obedience to what he claimed to be the will of God, it was obviously more difficult for those who followed him, especially those who had seen the Franciscan way of life only at second-hand. That was why it was essential to have a Rule and why that Rule had to be obeyed.

Blessed Francis [we are told], who observed the Holy Gospel perfectly and zealously, earnestly desired that all friars should observe the Rule, which itself is nothing other than a perfect observance of the Gospel; and he gave his especial blessing to those who are, and will be, zealous in this.

He used to tell his followers that our profession was the book of life, the hope of salvation, the pledge of glory, the heart of the Gospel, the way of the cross, the state of perfection, the key of paradise, and the compact of the eternal covenant. He wanted the Rule to be understood and accepted by all, and wished the friars to discuss it in their conferences, and meditate on it frequently by themselves, in order to remind them of their guiding vows. He also taught them that the Rule should be always before their eyes as a reminder of the life they should lead and had bound themselves to follow. And, in addition, he wished and taught the friars that they should die with it before them. (*S.P.* 76)

Obedience – to God, to the Gospel teaching, and to the ideals of St Francis as set out in the Rule – was essential if God's work was to be done; and Francis was determined to set an example which others could imitate.

As often as the severity of his life was reproved (writes Celano) he would reply that he had been given to the Order as an example, that, as an eagle, he might encourage his young ones to fly. (*2 Cel.* 173)

And it was through obedience that Francis found joy, the inner joy of knowing that he was doing the will of God.

Francis described this spiritual joy in the following way:

If the servant of God strives to obtain and preserve both outwardly and inwardly the joyful spirit which springs from purity of heart and is acquired through devout prayer, the devils have no power to hurt him, and they say: 'We can find no way to get at him or hurt him because this servant of God preserves his joy both in trouble and in prosperity'. But the devils are delighted when they discover means to quench or disturb the devotion and joy which springs from true prayer and other holy practices . . . Therefore, my brothers, since this spiritual joy comes from cleanness of heart and the purity of constant prayer, it must be your first concern to acquire and preserve these two virtues, so as to possess this inward joy that I so greatly desire and love to see both in you and in myself, and which edify our neighbour and reproach our enemy. For it is the lot of the devil and his minions to be sorrowful, but ours always to be happy and rejoice in the Lord. (*S.P.* 95)

Francis, therefore, liked his friars to go about showing

a sense of joy, the joy which comes from forgiveness of sins and dedication to the service of God and man. One of the nick-names which Francis gave to them was *joculatores Domini*, 'the Lord's minstrels'; and he liked to think of them going about the world singing songs to the glory of God and showing how joyful they were.

It would, however, be a mistake to think of St Francis as a jolly man, the sort who has a smile for everyone and who regards it as his mission to spread conviviality and happiness. Quite the opposite. It is true that Francis wanted his friars to look cheerful – 'Always do your best', he said, 'to be cheerful when you are with me and the other brethren; it is not right for a servant of God to show a sad or gloomy face to his brother or to anyone else.' But Brother Leo goes on to say:

> It should not be imagined that our Father, who loved dignified and sensible behaviour, wished this spiritual joy to be shown in levity or empty chatter, for these things are not evidence of spiritual joy, but of emptiness and folly. He greatly disliked laughter and idle gossip in a servant of God; in fact, he preferred him not to laugh, and to avoid giving others any occasion for hilarity. In one of his Counsels he gave an even clearer definition of the nature of spiritual joy in a servant of God, saying: 'Blessed is the Religious who has no pleasure or joy except in the most holy sayings and works of the Lord, and by these inspires men to the love of God in joy and gladness. And woe to the Religious who takes delight in idle and foolish talk, and by them provokes men to laughter'. (*S.P.* 96)

Francis himself was always far more likely to be found crying than laughing. It was, in fact, largely through constant weeping that, in later life, he lost his sight. As Bonaventura said:

He had attained extraordinary purity of soul and body, yet he never ceased from purifying his spiritual vision with floods of tears, and thought nothing of the fact that this was costing him his sight. (*Bon.* v, 8).

Yet the inner, spiritual joy was always there, the joy that triumphs over weariness and sickness, over the mockery and hostility of others, over misunderstanding and·betrayal on the part of his friends. In what is perhaps the most moving chapter of the *Little Flowers* we read as follows:

As St Francis went once on a time from Perugia to St Mary of the Angels with Brother Leo, in the winter, they suffered greatly from the severity of the cold; and St Francis called to Brother Leo, who was going on a little in advance: 'O Brother Leo, although the Friars Minor in these parts give a great example of sanctity and good edification, write it down and note it well that this is not perfect joy'. And having gone a little further, he called to him the second time: 'O Brother Leo, even though the Friars Minor should give sight to the blind, and loose the limbs of the paralysed, and though they should cast out devils, and give hearing to the deaf, speech to the dumb and the power of walking to the lame; and although – which is a greater thing than these – they should raise to life those who had been dead four days, write that in all this there is not perfect joy'. And going on a little while, he cried aloud: 'O Brother Leo, if the Friars Minor knew all languages and all the sciences and all the Scriptures, and if they could prophesy and reveal not only things in the future but the secrets of consciences and of men's souls, write that in all this there is not perfect joy'. Going still a little further, St Francis called aloud again: 'O Brother Leo, thou little sheep of God, even though the Friars Minor spoke with the tongues of angels, and knew the courses of the stars, and the virtue of herbs, and though to them were revealed all the treasures of the earth, and though they knew the virtues of birds and of fishes and of all animals and of men, of trees, also, and of stones and roots and waters, write that not in this is perfect joy'. And going yet a little while on the way, St Francis called aloud: 'O Brother Leo, even though the Friars Minor should preach so well that they should convert all the infidels to the faith of Christ, write that herein is not perfect joy'.

And as he spoke in this manner during two good miles, Brother Leo, in great astonishment, asked of him and said: 'Father, I pray thee, for God's sake, tell me wherein is perfect joy'. And St Francis replied to him: 'When we shall have come to St Mary of the Angels, soaked as we are with the rain and frozen with the cold, encrusted with mud and afflicted with hunger, and shall knock at the door, if the porter should come and ask angrily: "Who are you?" and we replying: "We are two of your brethren" he should say: "You speak falsely; you are two vagabonds who go about the world stealing alms from the poor; go your way"; and if he would not open the door to us, but left us without, exposed till night to the snow and the wind and the torrents of rain, in cold and hunger; then if we should bear so much abuse and cruelty and such a dismissal patiently, without disturbance and without murmuring at him, and should think humbly and charitably that this porter knew us truly, and that God would have him speak against us, O Brother Leo, write that this would be perfect joy. And if we should continue to knock, and he should come out in a rage, and should drive us away as importunate villains, with rudeness and with buffetings, saying: "Depart from this house, vile thieves; go to the poor-house, for you shall neither eat nor be lodged here"; if we should sustain this with patience, and with joy, and with love, O

Brother Leo, write that this would be perfect joy. And if constrained by hunger, and the cold, and the night, we should knock yet again, and beg him with many tears, for the love of God, that he would open to us and let us in, and he should say yet more angrily: "These are importunate rascals, I will pay them well for this as they deserve", and should come out furiously with a knotted stick, and seize hold of us by our hoods and throw us to the earth, and roll us in the snow, and beat us all over our bodies; if we should bear all these things patiently and with joy, thinking on the pains of the blessed Christ, as that which we ought to bear for his love, O Brother Leo, write that it is in this that there is perfect joy. Finally, hear the conclusion, Brother Leo: above all the graces and gifts of the Holy Spirit, which Christ has given to his friends, is that of conquering oneself, and suffering willingly for the love of Christ all pain, ill-usage and opprobrium and calamity; because of all the other gifts of God we can glory in none, seeing they are not ours, but God's; as said the Apostle: What hast thou that thou hast not received of God? And if thou hast received it of God, why dost thou glory as if thou hadst it of thyself? But in the cross of tribulation and affliction we may glory, for these are ours; and therefore, says the Apostle, I will not glory save in the cross of our Lord Jesus Christ'. (*L.F.* 8)

In spite, therefore, of all his troubles and tribulations, of the agony of his wounds, the pain of his sicknesses, and the sadness of his heart, Francis could say on his deathbed: 'I have done my duty; may Christ teach you yours'; and, as Celano tells us, 'he accepted death singing'.

FOR FURTHER READING

Paul Sabatier   *Life of St Francis of Assisi* (an English translation of the famous life by the French writer, published in 1894).

Fr Cuthbert   St Francis of Assisi (a standard life, first published in 1912).

G. K. Chesterton   St Francis of Assisi (a sketch rather than a formal life, but well worth reading).

Omer Englebert   St Francis of Assisi – a new translation by Eve Marie Cooper of a French life of the saint, with an excellent Bibliography of over 100 pages.

John R. H. Moorman   Saint Francis of Assisi (new edition, 1976).